A LOVE AFFAIR
—WITH—
FAILURE

DR. AKINTOYE AKINDELE | OLAKUNLE SORIYAN

A LOVE AFFAIR —WITH— FAILURE

WHEN HITTING BOTTOM BECOMES A LAUNCHPAD TO SUCCESS

ForbesBooks

Published by ForbesBooks, Charleston, South Carolina.
Member of Advantage Media Group.

ForbesBooks is a registered trademark, and the ForbesBooks colophon is a trademark of Forbes Media, LLC.

Printed in the United States of America.

10 9 8 7 6 5 4 3 2 1

ISBN: 978-1-955884-32-7
LCCN: 2022908359

Book design by Analisa Smith.

Since 1917, Forbes has remained steadfast in its mission to serve as the defining voice of entrepreneurial capitalism. ForbesBooks, launched in 2016 through a partnership with Advantage Media Group, furthers that aim by helping business and thought leaders bring their stories, passion, and knowledge to the forefront in custom books. Opinions expressed by ForbesBooks authors are their own. To be considered for publication, please visit **www.forbesbooks.com**.

We dedicate our book to the abiding grace of God ... and to the hope of greatness for the great destiny of our blessed continent, Africa.

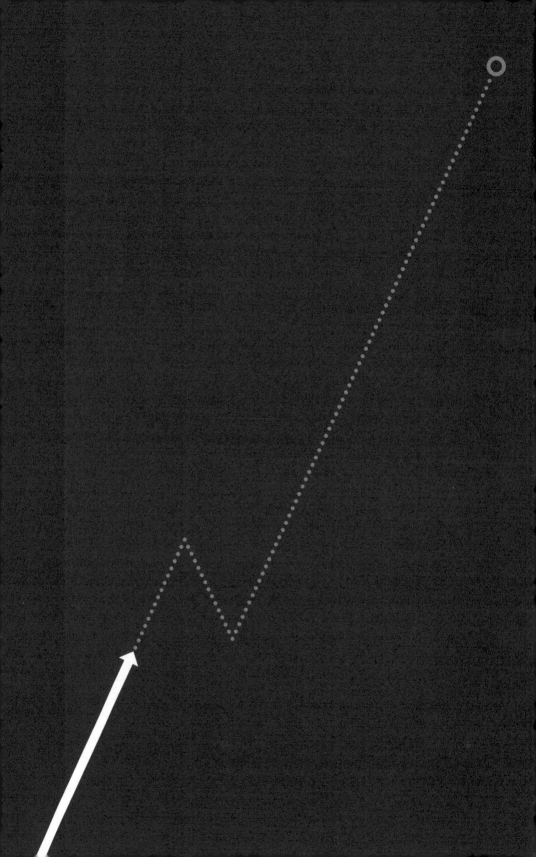

CONTENTS

FOREWORD

BY BISHOP T. D. JAKES, SR.

. . . .

The meandering path through the jungle of life is often filled with unexpected shadows, sharp jagged thorns, and the topography forward is often adorned with many rocks, ridges, and rubbish as we climb the mountains and ford the rushing streams that lead to the acquisition of your dreams. However, by the time an individual arrives at any modicum of success and stands in the clearing, which signifies clarity; many spectators and onlookers seem to think he is stepping into the brilliant effervescence of light and notoriety, tossed a dime in a wishing well, and magically achieved. But the truth of the matter is, there is no sunshine without rain, nor pleasure without pain. Failures and fallouts, setbacks, and detours are par for the course!

The battle-scarred hands of a warrior aren't ever inspected to assess how many losses preceded his victory. Instead, most "would be" leaders, trendsetters, and even giant slayers if they were undeterred by the failures and fallings that stimulate the soul to be a winner instead choose to dream wishfully and work whimsically, never knowing that failure is the chancellor of experience. It builds tenacity. Like the stumbling of a toddler's is the catalyst that strengthens the bones, fortifies the collaborative partnership causing nerves and muscles to engage for movement developing his equilibrium, failures help coordinate the balance he needs to stand.

Having built many businesses, spawned successful real estate businesses, founded schools and foundations, produced multiple television features, as well as production of films that built equity and created jobs, all while I pioneered a formidable church, I've failed my way forward through many experiences.

I've walked beside heads of state, presidents, and world leaders. One gets to know that the way up is down. The road to progress requires small steps. I am happy to lend my voice in preparing you for what's next. What Dr. Akindele and Olakunle Soriyan share in their groundbreaking book *A Love Affair with Failure* provides a fresh perspective for the entrepreneur, business person, or company leader. Their message is the elixir of truth that most never partake. If you are to be a winner, you must also be prepared to fail, fall, trip, and rise back up bloody but not beaten.

Dr. Akintoye Akindele and Olakunle Soriyan are merely scouts, guides who have persevered the vicissitudes of life and now leave us the clues and indisputable evidence that failure doesn't constitute defeat. I met Dr. Akintoye Akindele and Olakunle Soriyan in Dallas, TX, though they had both been listening to my teachings long before we met, Dr. Akindele in particular. Their brilliance couldn't be ignored. At first glimpse, we couldn't be more different. They are sons of the soil of Nigeria. And even though my ancestors hailed from West Africa in what is now called Nigeria, I was born and raised in America. Our languages and personal stories are as far apart as the waters that separated our homelands. And, though I grew up in a very modest environment, there was little synergism in our childhood experiences.

Dr. Akintoye Akindele, however, crosses me on a unique path. His religious affiliation is Muslim. I am a Christian and a Christian global voice at that! So, his theology was quite different from mine, yet our life's philosophy bore a stark resemblance. His compassion is unparalleled. But, his call to global development of the "least of these" challenges us all to transformative sociological strategies! Yet, standing with Dr. Akindele outside the 'Africa House,' an entrepreneurial nurturing and development center in Dallas, where he is Chairperson and his co-author is CEO, there was something providential about that moment. Dr. Akintoye Akindele seemed oddly familiar, the fire in his eyes and the stride in his gait all pointed toward purposeful and thoughtful reflection. When he shared his vision for all people but particularly the oppressed, it caught my attention. His passion for Black people, whether in Africa, the Caribbean, the United Kingdom, or the United States, was captivating. Our similarities about the care and wellbeing of oppressed people became the joint that welded this new and fascinating relationship. One turn of a ship's stern, one fastening of a shackle, one transaction of a slave trader, and he could've been me, and I might've been him. I leaned in with a keen curiosity. He was so excited I had to get him to speak slower, not wanting to miss anything he had shared. We both yearned to see those less fortunate be equipped with the necessary tools to make a viable and valued contribution to the entirety of the human race.

I believe very strongly that as a people, our shared goals, callings, and perspectives were to contextualize the right and relativity for Black people to walk shoulder to shoulder with all the humane accruements necessary to be uplifted. It is then and only then that the rotting stench of hatred and human depravity can begin to be quenched as we walk with God and in harmony with men. To be sure, we were meant to be our brother's keeper. Whatever we build must serve a higher purpose than ourselves. Wherever we go, we must be sure we bring someone with us who couldn't otherwise go. When our people become vested in equality and draped in justice, the world spins centered on the axis of equality. To starve us of that opportunity will only bring all of humanity into a famine that deprives the oppressed and distorts the oppressor.

Dr. Akintoye Akindele and Olakunle Soriyan are both culture shapers and influencers in their own rights, and as I engaged with them, it became increasingly clear that from our very different spheres of influence was a common drumbeat to add value to the human experience. It was a very similar need to provoke change. What we have in common is a passion for changing the world one life at a time. We recognize that the national GDP of any country cannot be calculated if the accountant doesn't aggregate the potential of human resources, deeming it more valuable than oil, gas, ivory, or even gold. I am counting on and counting up the wealth hidden inside of this progression.

One doesn't buy a real book. Truth is not for sale. Anything spent on wisdom and/or knowledge is an investment in oneself. The dividends are accrued over time, and the shares appreciate through the experiences we have, both good and bad. The incalculable wealth of a people lies in the realm of their potential to learn, adapt, and evolve as a species divinely endowed for the benefit of all others and to the glory of God Himself, who created us with creativity in our souls. It is when we see the wealth of our uniqueness, tabulating both our successes and our failures in the column of assets, that we become priceless pleasures of our creator. Indeed we add texture and tone to all humanity.

The brilliance of Dr. Akindele and his co-author has made their initiatives a global phenomenon. This brilliance is about to be downloaded into the hard drive of everyone who aspires to be more than their point of origin. I believe their writing is the catalyst of that point of view that makes us relentlessly committed to better!

Many years ago, I was blessed to adorn the cover of *Time* magazine. In bold letters, it read: IS THIS THE NEXT BILLY GRAHAM? While to be mentioned in the same breath with him was humbling, the goal was never to be the next Billy Graham. Who wants to be a cheap copy of a great original? Neither is the goal to be the next Mahatma Gandhi. It isn't to be the next Nelson Rolihlahla Mandela. We don't need another Dr. Martin Luther King, Jr. All of that has been done before. What the whole creation groans for, labors in travail for, is for you to be the next you!

How can I do that, you might ask? First of all, ask God to show you what His dream is for you, rather than showing Him what you have dreamed up for yourself. Secondly, surround yourself with others who are in hot pursuit of their destiny too. That is where reading leads the leader and feeds the feeder. Allow Akintoye and Olakunle to share their victories and defeats; their wisdom and the clarity they bring is born of them both. What I found amazing about this book is their transparency to show you their successes in context with their many failures. They assert they are inextricably connected. My hope is when you finish reading, you might pick up the dreams from the place of your failures and be willing to reevaluate them in the context of this eye-opening journey you are about to take with these very unique individuals! Perhaps it will unblock the dam of greatness that has paralyzed your mobility and invigorate you to reach beyond the breach, step over the potholes life has presented, and make it to the clearing. I can see the light up ahead. Get up now. It's time to cross the gulf, ford through the stream, discard the excuses, and fail your way forward!

The wisdom shared in this book is designed to feed the process that is a critical conduit that leads to the promise set before you. Before it's over, even you may find yourself hopelessly in love. Albeit, it will inevitably become "A Love Affair with Failure!"

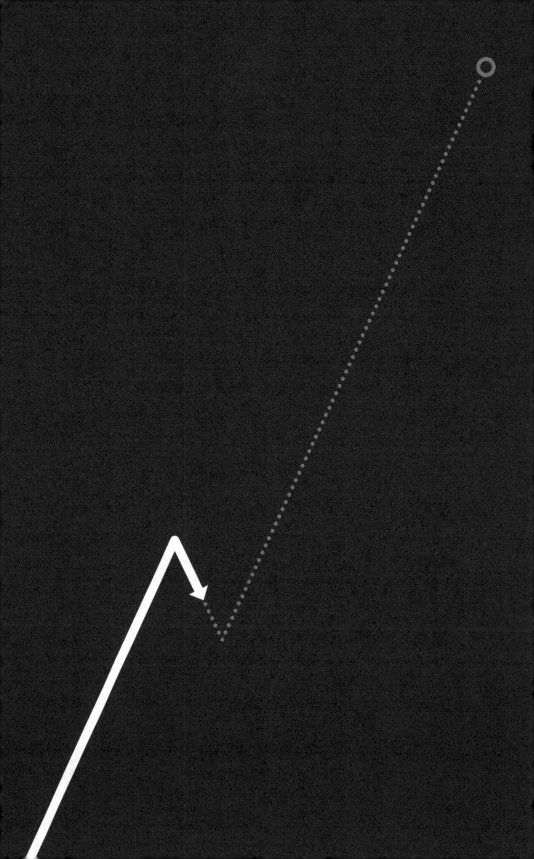

CHAPTER ONE

THE PROGRESS OF FAILING

. . . .

In 2016 a total of 462 ninth- and tenth-grade students participated in a study. Led by cognitive studies researcher Dr. Xiaodong Lin-Siegler of Columbia University's Teachers College, the study tested the effect of success stories on the motivation and performance of students. Divided into two groups, one set of students was given three stories about eminent scientists that described their intellectual struggles, personal failures, and repeated attempts at scientific discovery. The other set of students was exposed to stories of great scientific feats and pristine endeavors devoid of mistakes, much like the instructional material that appears in many scientific textbooks. The results ran contrary to conventional expectations.

The students who learned about the personal struggles and intellectual failures of scientists such as Albert Einstein and Marie Curie demonstrated marked improvements in learning and results, while the students who read only about scientific successes experienced declining grades. The results suggest the importance of reviewing our assumptions and beliefs about the impact of failing and the effect our ideas about failure have on our abilities and chances of succeeding. Failure holds a richer store of value than we imagine and plays a major role in guiding the route we take toward achieving our goals and attaining success.

Tons and tons of material has been written about what it takes and what it means to succeed, books spelling out specific steps, tomes pointing us to the great achievements of successful people—lone geniuses who, through sheer talent and hard work, invented the modern world, inspired corporations, and birthed great nations. But real life is less utopian. It is a messy affair riddled with mistakes, shortcomings, rejections, defeats, self-doubt, and more, all encoded with success. Today every creation deemed successful is composed of the aggregated results of things not going exactly as planned. Failure is the birthplace of success. Comfort is the mother of stagnation, and chaos is the father of change. From the chance occurrence of life in the universe, after billions of failed attempts over billions of years, to the basic comforts of our everyday existence, failure has an exceedingly strong track record of delivering success. In fact, if there is anything we should be learning, it is how to fail—and how to fail as often as necessary.

We set out to write this book because too many endeavors with potentially game-changing outcomes are short-circuited by the fear of failing. People with tremendous ideas are paralyzed by what-ifs, unable to see past the challenges of today. Yet the sure thing about the future is that it will happen one way or the other. The question is, are you positioning yourself for it? Or are you resting on your past successes or beating yourself up about your past failures? Are you feeling immobilized because of the fear you might fall flat on your face? Perhaps you will, but that won't be the end. The beauty of tomorrow is that it is filled with possibilities. It is a blank canvas, and you are the artist creating a masterpiece. So go ahead, dream, create, skill up, make an effort, take a chance, and try again and again; the universe listens eventually. Those who took the chance and executed are the ones who created the today we now know. And frankly, they are also the ones who dictate the terms of your current existence. How about you change that by creating the tomorrow you want to live in one effort at a time starting today?

Dr. Lin-Siegler's study shows that we have more to gain from normalizing failing than we do from avoiding it. But why is this so difficult? We have been conditioned at every level to associate failing with shame. This is why we are hard-pressed to admit mistakes, prone to hemming and hawing when we fall short because to fail is to be blamed.

A robust 2015 study carried out by Google on what makes for high-performing teams put psychological safety (an environment that makes team members feel safe in taking risks without feeling insecure or embarrassed) at the top of the list. The truth is there is momentum in refraining from employing paralyzing self-criticism and comfort in creating personal psychological safe havens that allow us to perceive undesired outcomes in more positive and empowering ways. To explain how to do this effectively, we must begin by debunking the myth of failure. There is actually no such thing as failure. Failure is an impossibility.

FAILURE IS AN IMPOSSIBILITY

Galileo died a failure—at least so it seemed at the time of his death. Having invented the thermoscope and an improved military compass, made significant scientific discoveries, theorized on a wide range of scientific curiosities, and put forward the basic principle of relativity, Galileo is considered by many to be the "father of modern physics," the "father of the scientific method," and the "father of modern science." But when he died, on January 8, 1642, he was a discredited heretic under house arrest.

Galileo's opposition to the Aristotelian geocentric idea that the Earth was the center of the universe pitched him against the orthodoxy of his day. Following Copernicus, he championed the belief that the Earth rotated daily and revolved around the sun, reinforcing his arguments in a 1632 treatise titled *Dialogue Concerning the Two Chief World Systems*. In February 1633 Galileo was summoned to Rome for having doubled down on his position, which had previously been declared by an inquisitorial commission as "foolish and absurd in philosophy, and formally heretical." On June 22 he was forced to recant and was placed under house arrest. He died a couple of years later, and that was that ... or was it?

By 1718 the ban on the reprinting of Galileo's works was lifted. In 1939 Pope Pius XII, in a speech to the Pontifical Academy of Sciences, described Galileo as being one of the "most audacious heroes of research ... not afraid of stumbling blocks and risks on the way nor fearful of the funereal monuments." On October 31, 1992, Pope John Paul II acknowledged the Roman Catholic Church's error in condemning Galileo for arguing that the Earth revolves around the sun. Years later in March 2008, the Pontifical Academy of Sciences contemplated a plan to honor Galileo with a statue of him inside the Vatican walls. The discredited polymath had been vindicated in death, his "foolishness" recast as wisdom. Hundreds of years after his death, Galileo's efforts yielded fruit, and the "failures" he was once ridiculed for were now considered groundbreaking successes.

There is no such thing as failure. For as long as life exists and time continues to be infinite, failure is an impossibility. As with Galileo it may take hundreds of years after you're dead and gone, but the universe listens, and efforts are ultimately rewarded.

There is a finality the word *failure* carries that is at odds with the human experience. Your story is an evolving thread of movement marked by fits and starts, but it doesn't end until you die. And even in death, it is still being written and rewritten.

Do you know that Vincent van Gogh, considered today to be one of the greatest artists who ever lived, is thought to have sold just *one* painting before he committed suicide in 1890, at the age of thirty-seven, because he considered himself a failure? Van Gogh was the quintessential tortured artist who struggled his entire life to make a living from his work. He was so prolific he is reputed to have created about 2,100 artworks, including oil paintings and drawings across a range of genres, including landscapes, still lifes, and portraits. But he was not commercially successful during his lifetime. In early 1890 he sold his painting *The Red Vineyard* for 400 Belgian francs to Anna Boch, the sister of his friend Eugène Boch, and shot himself seven months later, unhappy, poor, unsung. So if anyone can be considered a failure, it's Vincent van Gogh. But *was* he one? In 1990 one hundred years after his death, a van Gogh painting, *Portrait of Dr. Gachet*, sold for $82 million.

Who says you are a failure? It's nothing like that! There is a completely different story in all the efforts you are yet to take. What parameters are you using to define your output? Which lens are you deploying to view your input? On what stage are you showcasing your creation? Each effort or output is progress, even if the outcome isn't the desired one. And progress is success. No one can define your success or failure except *you*, and since failure is impossible, you can only succeed if you make an attempt. Your dreams, goals, and ambitions are unique to you. Why should you let the opinions of others define you, your goals, or your output?

We wrote this book because we do not believe in *failure*. We believe in *failing*. Failure is a destination; it is a windowless prison that confines, but it does not exist unless you accept that it does. Failing, on the other hand, is taking a journey of new knowledge and new beginnings. *Failure* is a noun. It attempts to define you by informing you that your unfortunate experience is the limit of how far you can go or how well you can do. Deep in the recesses of your soul, it shouts, "This is the best you can do! This is who you are!" Yet who you are cannot be defined by where you are now because life is not static. Your destiny is still playing out. There are infinite possibilities to what you can become.

Failing is not a noun; it is a verb. It is an evolution, a change from one state to another—an outcome from effort invested. It is a sign of progress, a transition into something better. It is a gift that unravels new ways of thinking, of doing, and of manifesting. Failing is how modern civilization was built—a litany of failed attempts morphing into something better and greater at the prodding of thinkers and doers who were not afraid to take a chance.

In the tension-soaked period leading up to World War I, metallurgist Harry Brearley was hard at work in his lab, trying to fashion improvements for guns. Bullets spinning through furrowed barrels tended to erode gun metals over time as they rubbed against their walls. Brearley was determined to develop a noncorrosive alloy that made for sturdier weapons. But months and months of dedicated work yielded one undesired result after another. All he had to show for his efforts was a pile of discarded metal unsuitable for his intended creation.

However, within the rubble of his failings, something stood out. He noticed a piece of metal that didn't oxidize. Exploring further, he discovered it also did not scratch. Practically useless for producing the guns he'd set out to make, his newly discovered "stainless steel" would prove crucial to the modern world, with game-changing effects in architecture, medicine, the arts, and the culinary world. Drone technology, with all its wide-ranging applications—from military operations, geomapping, filming, and shipping and delivery to rescue operations, healthcare, disaster management, and archaeological surveys—was invented on the failed technology of the now discarded Aerocycle, a "personal helicopter" built in the 1950s by the US military as an easy-to-operate, low-flying aircraft. Almost everything that has made our lives today infinitely better and more productive has a failed precursor. *So why are you afraid to fail?*

The idea that we are better and stronger when we shift our paradigm from failure to failing is significant to our individual and collective progress. We must be ready to unlearn everything we have learned about failure. In fact, everything we have been taught is the opposite of what we need to succeed. In a bid to protect the self-esteem of children, academic communities are increasingly designing grading systems that protect kids from failing, inadvertently teaching them that it is bad or shameful to fail and that failing is the opposite of succeeding, doing them a great disservice in the process. Real life throws punches. No matter how well you duck, you are going to get hit in the face, and if you're not mentally prepared for that, you are going to throw in the towel.

The truth is that we are all going to fail many times over. Some people will have safety nets by virtue of being born in a different country and/or to different parents with the resources to help them quickly rebound. Many will have to reach within, and this is what we want to help you do. The deeper levels of achievement, ones that produce happiness and allow for meaningful impact, are forged in the crucible of failing. You only have to know how to bounce back and how to do so stronger and better. Our great destinies will always demand that we develop a journey mentality, not a destination mentality. The critical difference is that while failure is a destination, failing is a journey. The fact that you failed means you made an attempt; you made an effort to crystallize something you imagined. The higher truth is that both attempts and efforts, regardless of their outcomes, are not wastes. They are manure.

> Both attempts and efforts, regardless of their outcomes, are not wastes. They are manure.

THERE IS NO WASTE IN THE UNIVERSE

"I never quit until I get what I'm after. Negative results are just what I'm after. They are just as valuable to me as positive results." These are the words of one of the nineteenth and twentieth centuries' most notable inventors, Thomas Edison, the "Wizard of Menlo Park." Edison had some of the greatest successes of his time chiefly because he failed more than most. Consider the scale of his operations. Edison, in the course of a lifetime, secured patents for 1,093 different inventions. In 1888 he wrote down 112 ideas in a single day. More than half of them failed. But he had become so prolific in extrapolating insight from unsuccessful attempts that he gave us the incandescent light bulb, the alkaline battery, the phonograph, the Dictaphone, the kinetoscope, and many more inventions. He founded more than one hundred companies and employed thousands of assistants, engineers, machinists, and researchers. It is estimated that by the time of his death, about $15 billion of the national economy was derived from Edison's inventions alone.

Perhaps in looking at his invention of the incandescent light bulb, itself a symbol of ideas, we gain some insight into what Edison was made of. The story is that he made one thousand failed attempts before he finally got the light bulb right, famously remarking, "I did not fail. I only found one thousand ways to not make a light bulb." Edison did not consider his unsuccessful efforts to be wasted. He considered them manure, fuel for growth.

There are things nature instinctively understands that have been nurtured out of us by learning and experience. Lions are incredibly skilled predators, but even in groups, they only succeed in a quarter of their hunts. However, you'll never find a despondent lion unwilling to hunt again because it failed a few times. Be as hungry to fail as Edison was. You need knowledge for the journey, and you need manure for growth. You only get them from failing. Failing is the universe giving you a gift. Every result you get from your effort is pointing you in a direction closer to your desired result. You must open your mind enough to read the tea leaves. The universe does not have waste. It has manure. These are timeless principles.

Kunle and I are veterans of failure. Between us are tons of failed ideas and businesses that expired in the heat of reality before they even got a chance to blossom. Nothing teaches success better than multiple failures. There is no better preparation for winning than losing. Every glory has stories you don't know about. Even many of the stars you see in the night sky are dead suns of other galaxies.

My first forays into business were unmitigated disasters. I tried selling sand and failed. Do you know how easy it is to sell sand? Practically all you need to do is go to a sand supplier, buy sand, take it where it is needed, and sell it! It is that direct and straightforward. Yet I failed at it. My next enterprise met the same fate. I opened a cybercafe with my brother. It was so unprofitable and incurred so much debt that it took two to three years of scheduled payments from our salaries at the time to offset it. I have been told I will never amount to anything and have been laughed at more times than I can count. The scars are real and remind me of where I am coming from and what I have survived, and they give me reasons to believe I will survive today's and tomorrow's battles.

When you fail enough times, you know all the ways to fail and how to avoid them, and then magic happens. Doors open. We have come this far and are still on the journey because none of our results have been wasted. They have served as manure, precious gifts that have translated into something beautiful. Yet just as we do not believe in failure, we also do not believe in success. We believe in *succeeding*. Remember, it is a journey, not a destination. The moment you think you have succeeded, you begin to plateau.

Toye cannot be more right about this. Think of some of the biggest businesses around many years ago. Where are they today? Remember Leventis? Kingsway? Okada Air? Bata? WorldCom? Arthur Andersen? Stein Mart? Henri Bendel? Pier 1 Imports? The Weinstein Company? We can go on and on. What about the numerous highly successful businessmen whose names were on the lips of many people and many publications back in the day? While we cannot definitively ascertain what led to their decline, the larger point we can make from this is that nothing is static—not failure, not success. There is no such thing as failure just as there is no such thing as success. Life is a battle for improvement. The universe, as intricately woven and balanced as it is, is constantly in motion, still unraveling. How many shots have you taken at your target? How many have you missed? Take another one.

Michael Jordan was one of the greatest basketball players in history. This is what he said: "I've missed more than nine thousand shots in my career. I've lost almost three hundred games. Twenty-six times I've been trusted to take the game-winning shot and missed. I've failed over and over and over again in my life. And that is why I succeed." This is how it works.

In 2008 I took one of the biggest gambles in pursuit of my dreams as an entrepreneur. My accomplishments prior to this were not minuscule. I had tried things and succeeded, and I'd coached many into their destinies. Everything we set out to do was well thought out. The fundamentals seemed right. Our products were tested and seemed fit for market. We had a solid team in place.

But the results were ridiculously far off the mark, much farther than we had hoped. We lost millions in investment and were millions more in debt. This was in Lagos, Nigeria; the lines of justice and equity were much blurrier than they are today. I was going from one police station to another as creditors attacked my fundamental human rights on a regular basis. I was dealing with an exposure of over $1 million in 2008 (of other people's money, not counting my own personal loss). It was hard to imagine surviving this ordeal, much less trying again. I was embarrassed on many levels that even those who were clearly trying to manage a reputation of foolishness themselves were offering me counsel. Yet try again I did. We shrunk our operation into something smaller but better, smarter, and wiser. And today it's much bigger. My efforts did not produce the results I intended, but they were manure.

WHAT IS HOLDING YOU BACK?

Greatness is not guaranteed, but you will never know until you try. In our observations of life and people and as we glean from personal experiences, we have identified six types of people in pursuit of their dreams: (1) people who are trying (that is, who are planning and taking steps toward their dreams); (2) those who are failing (the results are not going or have not gone the way they'd expected); (3) people who have achieved and are currently succeeding; (4) people who think it is a waste of time to try based on various theories, ranging from conspiracy to spiritual, (5) people who want to try but just cannot take the first step either because they're perfectionists or because they assume there are resources they need but do not have, and (6) people who do nothing in pursuit of their goals but who specialize in analyzing, criticizing, and judging the other five types of people, thinking themselves better.

The overwhelming conclusion in dealing with the wide range of people who fall within these six categories is that many people do not go after their dreams because of fear of failure. Let's be clear though; fear is a necessary thing. This is not exactly inspirational, but from mankind's early existence, fear has continued to alert us to the threat of harm, whether that harm is physical or psychological. Fear is a protective instinct that has preserved and, in some cases, advanced our species. We built houses to protect ourselves from our carnivorous cousins. We developed medicine to stave off disease and hold death at bay. Fear, when leveraged effectively, produces positive results. And since everyone is afraid of something, it simply demonstrates our humanity. It shows us we are human and lets us know an outcome exists that we do not want to experience and would rather avoid. It is a natural, powerful, and primal emotion. Fear evokes a universal biological response and a highly individual emotional response, but it becomes an irrational response when it moves us away from the path forward.

Think about it: why would you permit yourself to be afraid of what you do not know? You have not made an effort; you have not produced any result, positive or negative. All you have is a blank canvas and your imagination in a world where optimism is free and enthusiasm costs nothing. To allow fear to take hold of you is to be imprisoned by what should otherwise set you free: your mind. You may very well have failed in previous endeavors but not the one you are intending to embark upon now. Others may have failed in pursuing it, but they are not you. If anything, their failings provide insight into what you can do better. Their pain is not your pain, and you cannot afford to be paralyzed by proxy.

> To allow fear to take hold of you is to be imprisoned by what should otherwise set you free: your mind.

Knowing how something feels and understanding the potential it truly holds requires some degree of effort. Failing also requires effort. In fact, knowledge and failing are cousins. If you do not make the effort, you will never know. You will never know what not to do and how not to do it, and you'll never know what *does* work. You cannot learn how to be a great driver by simply watching somebody else drive. You have to get behind the wheel yourself at some point. You might very well make a few wrong turns and earn the vehicle a few bruises, but with each effort comes consciousness and knowledge. Increase this store of knowledge with repeated efforts, and you are closer to your desired outcome.

Every failed attempt increases what we call your *knowledge capital*. And with every failing, you make a deposit in what we call your *knowledge and experience bank* (KE bank). As you build this KE bank, you get closer to having all the knowledge and experience you need to achieve your goals. In other words, repeated failing grows your KE bank balance by growing your knowledge capital and moving you closer to your goal.

Science cannot determine how many times one must try and fail before achieving one's goal. Three strikes, and one person hits gold. It's forty strikes for another. Too bad if he stops hitting at thirty-nine. It all depends on various factors, from market dynamics to information and resource availability. Quantum efforts vary, but the universe does not bend. Things take the time they need, and after repeated efforts, magic happens. You may be deemed "lucky" or an "overnight success" by those who do not realize or appreciate the time, effort, and commitment you invested.

The thinking here is that if success requires knowledge and knowledge requires failing, having a fear of failure is having a fear of success. It does not matter if your goal is to be an executive at a firm, to start your own firm, to be a great artist or athlete, to be the best professional in your area of core competence, or to just be happy. Whatever succeeding means to you, you are going to have to be knowledgeable to attain it. Beyond the secondhand knowledge you can glean from books or any other store of information, you are going to have to invest effort in trying, and some of those efforts will not pan out as expected.

As entrepreneurs and teachers, Kunle and I both have the rare privilege of being at the front seat of an emerging Africa—an Africa that's shooting for the moon faster than the world is ready for. This forward momentum is driven by young, hungry entrepreneurs with bold ideas and the tenacity to achieve them. From Nigeria to Kenya to South Africa and the Black diaspora, we have invested in and are continuing to invest in the change makers of tomorrow. One thing is sure: many of these individuals will change the narrative of Africa, and many of them will experience significant setbacks, heart-crushing failings, and sink-or-swim moments that will go down in the annals of history, depending on how they respond. Our goal is to ensure they respond effectively. And this is, in part, why we have written this book. If you are on your journey, keep going. If you are yet to start perhaps because you think your idea does not have a fighting chance, *start*. Come, let's take this journey together. The universe is waiting.

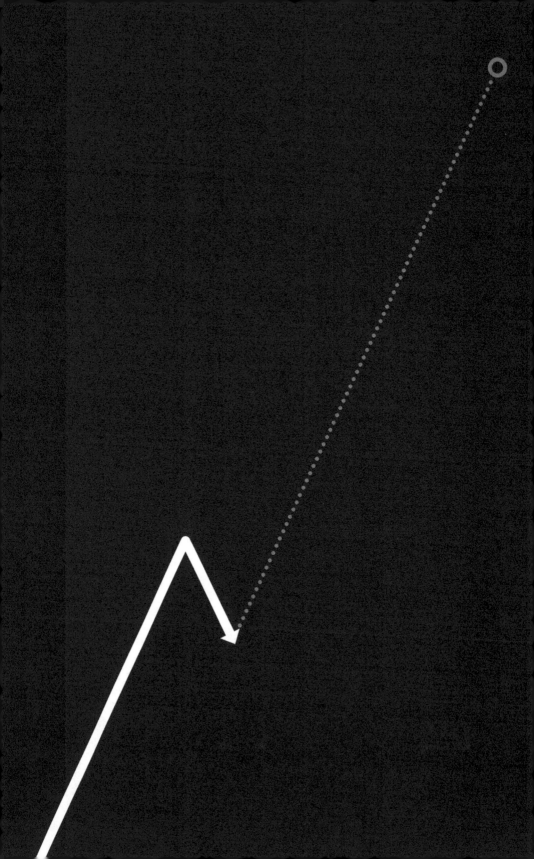

CHAPTER TWO

FAILING IS BEAUTIFUL

. . . .

Some of my best success stories have come from failing. My earliest taste of failure occurred around thirty-seven years ago. I was a bright young lad who outsmarted most of his peers in primary school to stay at the top of his class. My parents were cheerleaders and disciplinarians who expected nothing but outstanding results. And all through primary school, I never disappointed. My smooth transition into secondary education was considered a given. Buoyed by their confidence in me, I was enrolled by my parents to take five common entrance examinations to some of the top federal schools on offer at the time. My real journey was about to begin. And it turned out to be a baptism in failing. One by one the results came back, and they were anything but what we expected. I failed four out of the five—all my top choices included. My parents were disappointed and livid, and I will never forget my father's response in one instance.

One of the schools I had applied to and for which I failed the entrance exam was the Nigerian Air Force Secondary School. Only applicants who passed the examinations were scheduled for the next phase, an interview with the school's admissions board. But on the day of the interviews, my father—in a sheer burst of persistence and genuinely unable to believe or accept that his brilliant son did not pass an exam he'd said was easy—threw me into his car, drove me to the school, and requested they review the results again, as there must have been an error. He insisted I be interviewed, and his refusal to take no for an answer was one of the many lessons I would learn from him. The school eventually agreed, and I was interviewed. It was an august panel peopled with stern-looking academics. I stammered my way through with as much confidence as an unprepared ten-year-old could muster. I wish I could say I passed, but I didn't. I failed the interview, to my father's consternation.

Humbled by my failures and with all hope seemingly lost, just before the end of the summer of 1984, I received an admission letter to the Nigerian Navy Secondary School, Ojo. It is a great institution, one in which the Nigerian government invests significant resources to nurture young minds into future leaders. Now let us pause and review this series of events in the life of this ten-year-old boy. The Nigerian Navy Secondary School's examination was one of the toughest exams I took at that time. I remember clearly how difficult it was, but it was also the *last* exam of the five entrance examinations I took. By the time I was taking the Nigerian Navy Secondary School's exam, I had taken four other entrance tests, made mistakes, learned from them, and had gotten so good that the toughest test—which I took last—was the one I passed. The interesting thing was a few of my friends and classmates who passed the other entrance examinations did *not* pass the Nigerian Navy Secondary School's exam. So at the age of ten, I was lucky to have learned some important life lessons. Three key lessons stand out.

The first lesson was that my failed attempts at passing previous tests made me better, allowing me to pass the toughest test. The more I failed, the better I became, and I eventually succeeded in getting into the school that gave me what is arguably my strongest foundation as a person. The second lesson focuses on the power of persistence and belief. Seeing my father make his case to the Air Force Secondary School board and, in so doing, affording me another shot was priceless. Whether the school board realized the possibility of error in the results or was amused by his arguments or was simply impressed by his confidence in my abilities, the impossible happened, and I was granted an interview. The third lesson was that all my failures prepare me for the stage that life has set for me—that dream, that goal, that vision.

It was love at first sight with the Nigerian Navy Secondary School: the uniform, the school facilities, the neatness and carriage of the naval officers, the exclusivity of getting selected to take the test, and the overall ambience of the school complex. It was the school of my dreams. It was the school I wanted. It was new, fresh, impressive, and exclusive. If I had passed all five exams, I would still have chosen Nigerian Navy Secondary School. Dreams are realized when effort is matched with persistence, continuous improvement and learning, and hard work. The universe listens.

Few things could have prepared me for the life ahead like that school did. The Nigerian Navy Secondary School gifted me not only with lifelong lessons in discipline and excellence but also with some of the best friendships and networks, all of which have contributed significantly to a string of successful endeavors. And by the way, years later, in a beautiful twist of fate, I married the daughter of one of the interviewers at the Nigerian Air Force Secondary School, whose entrance exam I failed—and my life couldn't have been made any better.

What Kunle and I can tell you for certain is that nothing grounds us in reality as much as failing does. Success is a lousy teacher. You are most likely to fail after you have been successful because success makes you vulnerable to your ego, and there is no greater mountain upon which to plateau than your ego. Wins can be anchors or launch pads. After a journey, a ship anchors (a win). Then it must either sail again (try again through being vulnerable and taking risks) or stay at the dock. But a ship was made to sail, not be docked permanently. No win is permanent. Risk-taking is part of the process. You have to keep moving.

> Nothing grounds us in reality as much as failing does. Success is a lousy teacher.

To be grounded in reality is to also know that efforts are fundamental to human progress. Stasis is what nature abhors. The universe is in constant motion. It doesn't stop because of a seemingly failed attempt. Rain simply falls, whether on a park bench or in a field. It might land on hard ground or water a seed in a good soil, producing a plant that may still die in its youth. But the rain does not relent. It simply falls, time and again, in an unending cycle.

Science makes us understand that evolution adapts by repeating errors. Gene variations occur without cognizance of previous attempts. When the DNA copy of a bird, for example, creates a variation—for example, a longer beak—it does so without being conscious that these features might have been tried before—unsuccessfully or otherwise. It is blind to previous failures; it simply repeats. And what failed to become a beneficial trait generations ago may become one today. The environment changes. And where, by natural selection, a shorter beak was once preferred, a longer one may now offer an advantage. So part of the beauty of nature is its consistency, even in the face of what might seem like failure. Eve Fairbanks, in her essay "Why Failure Can Be a Good Thing, Even When We Don't Learn from Our Mistakes," puts it beautifully:

> If ever you doubt that nature loves futility and failure, go to the sea. Walking in the surf last month in South Africa, I saw a plethora of little blue snails burrowing into the sand. The precision and the effort they put into it was amazing: first the pinprick of a hole in the beach, then a wriggle until only the round ends of their shells peeked out. They looked snug, at home. And then, of course, the wave: it demolished all their effort, sending them tumbling back and leaving them squirming, slimy foot upturned, in the receding surf. Repeat. Every effort they made was repulsed, and still they turned themselves over and persisted in rooting into the sand.
>
> I wondered if their efforts had some hidden purpose. I asked a pair of marine biologists: Hunger, they suggested, or the drive for shelter. But whatever their goal, the fact remained that they were overturned over and over, and tried again and again, in a perfect cycle of failure and desire. It was a reminder that Nature doesn't operate according to the four-hour workweek, the laws of maximum efficiency and effectiveness, whereby every misstep and wrong choice is a source of shame. On the contrary: mistakes combat stasis; missteps yield evolution; a thousand seeds drift in the wind that never take root, and those that take root crumple again in the hurricane.

My experience is not far different from Toye's. I was in high school at the tender age of nine, and by age fourteen, I was sitting for my final exams (the Senior School Certificate Exams with the West African Examinations Council). I was the star of my family and a beloved member of my community. But I was also in a boarding school at the tender age of three—a mere child, too young to deal with the weighty experiences of boardinghouse life in 1980s Nigeria. In the early '80s, high school students, such as Stephen Keshi and Henry Nwosu, were playing for national soccer teams in Africa. My school's soccer team also had boys who—to a boy under age ten as I was—looked like mature adults. So naturally, I was bullied, so much so that I hated showing up among my peers. I was so small they nicknamed me Atom. As a coping mechanism, I developed a mental and attitudinal posture that helped me socially but that shut me in my own world and made me overdependent on myself and my talents.

As a high school student at age nine, I was certainly smart, but I was not studying. Somehow I got away with this until my senior year, in which talent was clearly not enough. I had to study to succeed, but I just couldn't do so. I failed my final exams, along with a number of retakes, and could not gain admission to a university until four years after high school. The failure was a disappointment to my parents, a big blow to the adults of my neighborhood, and a trolling tool in the hands of my peers, as I never heard the last of it. It was torture to my soul and an unrelenting noise in my own head.

The idea that I was a failure didn't leave me for a while. I went on to spend twelve years at a university taking a four-year course. I just could not do enough to graduate until twelve years after I began. In those twelve years, I could very well have gotten a bachelor's degree, two master's degrees, and a doctorate. Each of those years was torture, like weights holding me down on a daily basis. During the final eight years of the twelve, I started a refuse collection business; it failed. I transitioned to a pest control business; it also did not work. I then got into the food business, and while it did not go badly, it still did not represent the outcome that my efforts deserved. All the while, accusing tongues and pointing fingers were working feverishly against me, deeming me no good. I became something of a proverb and a byword in my neighborhood, as parents used me as an example not to be followed when admonishing their children.

Today, though, I have hired four of my mates who managed to move ahead while I was struggling in school. I live a life that thousands across the world would want to lead, even for a second. On many levels I feel that if I were to have to live life all over again, I would do it the same way. I would fail everywhere I have failed in this life, trusting that it would bring me back to where I am today, because truly I have no regrets. Failure has been a signpost, a map of self-discovery. If all my failures were taken away, I sincerely do not know who I would be. There is no way I could define the Olakunle Soriyan I know today if I did not have the privileges of both the fortunes and the misfortunes of my history. I was failing, I am still failing, and I will continue to fail, but I am moving forward and progressing all the time and building more and more peace. It is not an act of genius; it is simply the way of the universe. God designed it so.

Looking back at the early and persistent failures that marked my journey, alongside Toye's beautifully told personal history and early experiences as a young lad leaping into a new phase of life, I believe there are two principles to keep in mind. One is that sometimes an attempt is its own reward. We have been thrust into an expanding universe, and missteps are part of the evolutionary process. The second principle is that efforts yield positive outcomes that are sometimes shielded from us at the outset.

In his hotly debated essay "The Principle of the Hiding Hand," the late economist and thinker Albert Hirschman described, with a very interesting anecdote, the surprising benefits of not having the full picture before making an attempt. As the story goes, the Karnaphuli Paper Mill, located in what was then East Pakistan, was built to become one of the largest and most profitable paper mills in the region. In order to make it work, the mill was sited close to the vast bamboo forests of the Chittagong Hill Tracts. But shortly after the mill commenced operation, it ran into unexpected trouble: the bamboo flowered and died. This was a rare phenomenon then, but it's now known to recur every fifty years or so. There was no way it could have been effectively envisaged. Dead bamboo was useless for pulping; it fell apart as it was floated down the river. This grave miscalculation was set to throw the new multimillion-dollar industrial plant into jeopardy and bankrupt its owners. But what happened was a master class in adaptability, and the results were phenomenal.

Rather than sit, sulk, and trade blame, the owners swiftly responded to the crisis. They found new ways to bring in bamboo from villages throughout East Pakistan using the country's many waterways, opening a new supply chain as a result. They also started a research program to find faster-growing species of bamboo to replace the dead forests, and they planted an experimental tract. They found other kinds of lumber that worked just as well, and the result was that the plant was blessed with a far more diversified base of raw materials than was initially imagined. If poor planning had not led to the crisis at the Karnaphuli plant, the mill's operators would never have been forced to be creative, and the plant would not have been nearly as valuable as it became.

The beauty of failing is in the possibilities birthed by each attempt at something audacious. Everything great that has ever been built has been the result of an attempt. Your very life is the product of a sperm's attempt to fertilize an egg. Yet attempts in themselves are the fruits of a latent force: curiosity.

THE CURIOSITY DNA

Kunle and I are spiritual people. At the core of who we are and all we do is the idea that possibilities are too endless in the human zone for us to indulge the certainty that a God does not exist. In our conclusion, He does exist, and He rules in the affairs of humans. For us, though, no part of spirituality, as we understand it, disagrees with the basic tenets of science such that a divergence of views in a few areas will cancel the commonalities that align spirituality and science. One of these commonalities is the force of curiosity.

Curiosity is the very spark of human existence. Scientists believe our world willed itself into being as a speck of matter wanting to be more and took a shot at multiple life-forms starting more than four billion years ago. Creationists insist the universe was summoned out of darkness by a restless God who fleshed out its design and, curious to see what man would make of it, placed him at the center of it. Driven by latent curiosity, man, in turn, reached out for the knowledge of good and evil. Whatever you believe, one thing is clear: everything that exists is the product of curiosity—a desire to increase knowledge, create meaning and purpose, birth newness, and find the why of things, the hows, the wheres.

Curiosity is a function of restlessness, and restlessness is the motion that creates an attempt. Every time an attempt is made, possibilities are born, multiple outcomes resulting from exerted effort(s). Attempts that meet the goal of the question(s) asked are labeled successes. Those that do not are undesired results, not failures, just undesired results. In some cases they turn out to be signposts, redirecting and refining our attempts. In other cases they produce a different dimension of success.

When Will and John Kellogg placed a bowl of wheat on the stove in 1894, what they wanted to do was make some dough as part of their quest to provide healthier dietary options for the patients in the sanitarium they ran together. Distracted by other pressing matters, Will forgot about the wheat and returned hours later to find it stale. In a frantic effort to salvage it, the brothers forced the stale wheat through rollers, hoping to extract some semblance of dough. What they got instead were crisp flakes that tasted unlike anything they knew, an undesired result that would go on to become the world's number one breakfast cereal: cornflakes.

> Curiosity is a strong counterpoint to fear. Fear impedes your drive or desire to try. Curiosity releases it.

What are you curious about? What attempts are you making? How are you evaluating the results of those attempts? Curiosity is a strong counterpoint to fear. Fear impedes your drive or desire to try. Curiosity releases it. Fear envisages a myriad of things going wrong. Curiosity is open to surprise, open to multiple possibilities and outcomes. It's not ashamed of undesired results, as it converts them into positive lessons. Curiosity is the playground of discovery. Practically every great invention that has advanced the cause of mankind is the product of curiosity, the result of restless thinkers who were not afraid to try and try again.

You were born with an impulse to seek knowledge and try things out. Studies show that children are in a constant state of questioning because they have not lost their ability to be surprised. They are likely to keep probing until they arrive at understanding. When they hold certain ideas that turn out to be wrong, they try to find out why and revise their thinking. Do not lose your sense of surprise. Do not lose your curiosity. Safeguarding and encouraging curiosity is a matter of survival on every level.

Societies advance in direct proportion to their support for scientific and medical research, support for the arts, free expression, and sustenance of libraries, in other words support for curiosity. The ancient Greek civilization had an impact on human progress like few other periods of history. The ancient Greeks are credited for daring to go in directions previous civilizations could not. They advanced mathematics, broke ground in science and medicine, redefined the arts, encouraged philosophy, documented astronomy, introduced the world to geometry, invented modern-day democracy, and started the Olympics. Think Aristotle, Plato, Archimedes, Pythagoras, and Socrates. The Greeks' unrivalled contributions to global history and modernity were no fluke. It was the result of abundant curiosity. They created and nurtured an environment that encouraged inquiry, questioning, debates, ideas, and different ways of looking at the world. When faced with unexplained phenomena and problems, they did not turn to religion as a way to cope with mystery as many civilizations before them did. They investigated and tried to solve their problems.

In fact, scientific inquiry as we know it today took off from the ancient city of Miletus, where the Greeks discovered that their harbor had become impassable. The typical recourse would have been to blame the gods, but they did not. They asked why. After probing into the matter, they discovered that silt from up the river had caused the blockage. Thus, science was born. The Greeks, of course, had religion, but it existed side by side with freedom of thought. As a result they bequeathed to us a tested formula for building great societies: restless, driven curiosity leading to experiments that birth multiple possibilities.

Perhaps China's recent history provides us with equal insight into the centrality of curiosity in advancing society and upholding the common good. When the Chinese civil war birthed the People's Republic of China in 1949, the ancient country was an ambitious and complicated state at odds with itself. It is important to note that China was one of the world's first civilizations. Successive ruling dynasties gave us what the Chinese proudly refer to today as the Four Great Inventions: the compass, gunpowder, papermaking, and printing. However, future centuries of internal conflict and foreign imperialism would contribute to significantly weakening the country.

When Mao Zedong came to power on October 1, 1949, it was on the urgent promise of restoring the country's greatness. But what we remember most today about Mao's ambitions were the disastrous ways he went about fulfilling this promise—most notably his initiation of the Cultural Revolution. When Mao launched his revolution in May 1966, it was to rid the republic of "old customs," "old habits," "old culture," and "old ideas." But what followed, ironically, was the shutting down of schools and universities, the transformation of large swathes of young people into unthinking and violent apparatchiks, the public humiliation of intellectuals and voices of dissent, and ultimately the deaths of what historians estimate to be between five hundred thousand and one million people. Mao's avowed commitment to restoring China's greatness was dead on arrival because he stifled curiosity, unlike his successor, Deng Xiaoping, whose reforms included opening China up to the rest of the world, encouraging curiosity, investing in technology, and setting the republic on the path of economic greatness.

To shut down curiosity and the active exploration of ideas is to shut in the potential of the people and of society at large. This is why Africa's emerging, young dreamers are the change makers of today and tomorrow. These restless denizens are daring or solve age-old problems in new ways, harnessing the power of all the technology available to them, and putting the world on notice. What we must do at every level of society—from public policy to private facilitation to parenting—is create an environment that encourages more and more young people to question, probe, and explore ideas, backed by unrelenting capital that believes and invests in their ability to deliver long-term value.

Curiosity leads to relentlessness, which leads to effort, which leads to possibilities. There is no other way to create the lives, organizations, and nations we want. There are still so many unanswered questions out there, and if there is anything we know about human history, it is that the universe answers when we ask and ask again. We have come all the way from rubbing two stones together to produce fire to landing humans on the moon. Much of human progress depends on courageous leaps of the imagination. It depends on audacity, on embracing the beauty of failing and all the wonderful things that emerge when we try. The world would be a much poorer place if we limited ourselves to the knowledge available to us. To go further we must ask bigger and more daring questions, and we must follow them up with actions. When those actions do not produce the results we envisioned, we will gain knowledge, new ideas about how to try again. This is the beauty of failing. Empires are built on questions, not answers.

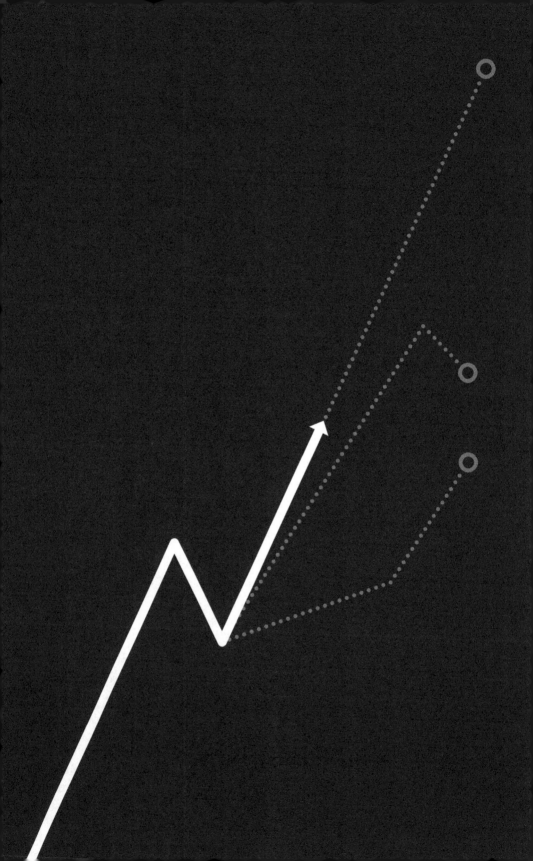

CHAPTER THREE

THE RIGHT TO CHOOSE YOUR JOURNEY

. . . .

Everyone is on a journey. Since birth, we've all been on a wild adventure through the hills and valleys of life, beckoned by wide-open fields of promise. Armed with manuals and road maps, along with formal and informal bodies of knowledge handed to us through time, we follow trails and beat paths. Our journeys are wholly unique but united by a universal yearning to make something meaningful of our lives. Perhaps the most underrated gift at our disposal is the power we each have to decide our destiny. We are typically blinded to this by preordained limitations, such as race, gender, geography, and social class. Time has shown us over and over again that no matter where we come from,

> **Perhaps the most underrated gift at our disposal is the power we each have to decide our destiny.**

regardless of the limitations of our backgrounds, we can rise up through the coalescent forces of grace, faith, and courage. This is an empowering realization to attain, and it is true.

There is no force within the realm of matter strong enough to hold back a person determined enough to change his or her fortune. We strongly believe that all human beings come equipped with the capacity to define their own reality, choose their own variables, and live life on their own terms. One of the most powerful books ever written is the 1946 bestseller *Man's Search for Meaning* by Holocaust survivor Viktor Frankl. Frankl's central theme is wrapped up in his belief that "[e]verything can be taken from a man but one thing: the last of the human freedoms—to choose one's attitude in any given set of circumstances, to choose one's own way." And it starts with a dream.

The concept of dreaming has made the rounds within the self-help circuit to such an extent it has become cliché. But its power is no less potent. When we do not dream, we start nothing. Dreams are alternate realities accessed through the imagination. It is, however, true that the inner workings of creating your own reality can be quite a daunting endeavor because it is often at odds with the challenging circumstances in front of you—the "reality" you can see and feel. A dream offers us a second sight, multiple possibilities at zero cost. Your imagination is an inexhaustive resource freely afforded to you by the miracle of life. A 2018 brain imaging study led by University of Colorado, Boulder, and Icahn School of Medicine at Mount Sinai researchers confirms that our imaginations are neurological realities that affect our real-life experiences. In other words, reality is a malleable construct, and you can remake it starting from within.

For years psychologists have used a technique called cognitive reframing to help people caught in the web of a depressing reality.

Cognitive reframing hinges on changing our inner narrative—the stories we have come to believe about ourselves, the world, and other people. Our lived experiences are so intensely personal they affect the unique lens through which we view the world. As we go through life, we encounter negative experiences that linger with us and sometimes entrench narratives that hold us back. This is why people who try and fail, whatever the endeavor, find it difficult to try again because they associate that attempt with failure and how it made them feel. But thoughts are not facts. The past is a store of knowledge and a sophisticated view of it is a vital resource for creating the future. By switching our thinking and reframing the failed attempt as a data point, as feedback, as knowledge, we become empowered to try again—and try again *better*.

People say life is filled with mountains and valleys. This may be true, but we must also remember that mountains are tall. We keep climbing. Sometimes we slip, take a wrong step, and fall down, but we haven't encountered a valley. It is simply an adjustment. It is us taking a rest from climbing and then continuing to climb as soon as we're up to it. This slight change of narrative makes a huge difference in the journey of life.

Try the "yes, but ..." approach. Yes, I am down, but I am only taking a rest, and I will climb again. Yes, this did not work out as planned, but I have learned a better way to approach it next time. And then get out of your head a bit. Make a multisensory effort. Look at your circumstances as they are in the present. Then reframe them in your mind. Write down an alternative view of the situation and what you want that to be. Document your dreams if you can, but do keep the right frame that aligns to what the universe promises you. Improvement and betterment are promises of a universe that is in itself a product of possibilities. Guaranteed positive outcomes exist for each one of the billions of people on the face of the planet, but it is also up to each to lean into this truth. Dreams are birthed in the mind, but they die there as well without strategic action. So reframe. Document. And then act. Your journey is defined by the steps you take.

CONNECTING THE DOTS

Traveler, there is no road;
you make your own path as you walk.
As you walk, you make your own road,
and when you look back,
you see the path.

—ANTONIO MACHADO

The paths that define our journeys in life are retrospective. When you were born, nobody handed you a picture and said, "This is your future, and this is the path you take to get there." There is actually no such thing as a future. Whatever you think the future is, when you get there, you will call it "today." Today was once the future, and today is all there is. The steps you take in the present create the possibilities that define your subsequent results. Our lives are like a series of dots that when connected, over time, form a picture of who we are, what we achieve, and who we become. But how can you connect dots you have not laid, and how do you lay dots?

You lay dots by taking chances. Each step in the direction of your dream is a dot plotted forward, forming a path that is only visible when you look back. To be clear, the beauty of dots is that they are never clear. You never really know where the chances you take will lead you, but you find the courage to take them anyway. Some of the chances you take and some of the dots you lay might look like errors and might be painful to pursue, but take them anyway. They are the tapestries of your success.

The eventual outcome of your life is the straightest line in a scatter diagram. A scatter diagram is a mathematical tool used to study the correlation between two variables. You have one variable on an X axis and another on a Y. Numerical data represented by dots are then used to explore the relationship between both variables, and a line is used to connect them. The better related the variables are, the tighter their correlation to the line. Think of every step you take in the pursuit of an idea, a vision, or a cause you believe in as a dot interacting with the variables of your life. The fewer dots you lay, the fewer chances you get at a tight correlation to a line. When a move you make goes as planned, your line plots upward; when it does not, it plots downward. Over time through consistency and the guidance of practice, they average out.

The "bottom line" is take every chance you get until you become better at failing and firmer at laying your dots. Also, remember that if you do not lay dots, life will lay them for you. You can either be the captain of your ship or be tossed to and fro by every wind of doctrine and chance. A ship in harbor, as they say, is safe, but that is not what ships are built for. Ships are made for venturing, turbulent seas be damned.

In November 1990, fifty-year-old Bill Irwin from Burlington, North Carolina, completed his thru-hike of the 2,167-mile Appalachian Trail to the stunned applause of admirers who followed his journey from across the country. What made Irwin's feat a national media event was not just his age or the estimated one thousand times he fell, the cracked ribs and hypothermia he suffered as he braved mountains and rivers, or the fact that he did not use a map or compass. What astounded everyone was the fact that he was blind, and all he had with him was his German shepherd, Orient.

Bill Irwin was not born blind, but his life had been a difficult one. His first four marriages ended in a divorce, and by his own admission, he was an absentee father with a drinking problem. "When I was a sighted person, I was an alcoholic, a dropout as a husband and father, a guy who lived only for himself," he said. In 1976 Irwin lost his sight completely, eight years after doctors had removed his left eye following a malignant melanoma misdiagnosis. His smoking and drinking worsened as did his relationships, but one day, he decided to turn it all around. Bill entered therapy, reconciled with his family, and began plotting a different set of dots.

His decision to take on the Appalachian Trail was also a stab at self-redemption, an audacious attempt at rewriting his history in the face of his many failures. Strapping on a sixty-pound backpack and adhering to a rigidly set timetable, the blind hiker embarked on his new journey. Discouraged, beaten, stressed, strained, fallen, blind Bill Irwin persisted. Along the way he would talk to other hikers, play with little children, wash his clothes at local Laundromats, and shop at small stores, dogged all the way by television cameras and mixed opinions about his chances of success.

On November 21, 1990, Irwin—kneeling at the finish line and singing "Amazing Grace"—became the first blind man to thru-hike the Appalachian Trail. In 1992 he published the best-selling memoir *Blind Courage,* and what a story it turned out to be. In it he summed up his life in the words of Paul the Apostle. "We walk by faith and not by sight." Irwin went on to become a sought-after motivational speaker and family counselor. Orient, his German shepherd, became the subject of a children's book titled *Orient: Hero Dog Guide of the Appalachian Trail.*

You have to believe in yourself enough to take chances. You can write and rewrite your history as well as route and reroute your journey by stepping in the direction of your dreams. What would you build if you were not afraid? Attempt it. What if it fails? Well, consider that fact and try again. The dots connect into greatness in favor of the bold.

When I left Obafemi Awolowo University, Ile-Ife, with a degree in chemical engineering, my goal was to get a job at one of the top private oil and gas firms. After unsuccessful attempts at gaining employment with Shell, Mobil, and even Flour Mills of Nigeria, I began my career as a workingman at the Nigerian National Petroleum Corporation (NNPC). It was a low-paying job with the languid pace of the Nigerian Civil Service. My starting salary equated to US$7 a month. After all my education and good grades, that was the only job I was offered. Imagine—after more than fifteen years of quality education at the top schools in Nigeria, my earning reality was US$7. The operative word here is *reality*—not *potential* or *capacity*—earning *reality.*

So obviously, I was eager and desperate to leave. I wanted something more financially rewarding and intellectually challenging. This was the mid-1990s; the Cold War was over, the world was in the fever of an economic boom, the millennium beckoned, and here I was, with a US$7 monthly salary. My reality was unacceptable, and I had to find a way to change it and redirect my future.

I reviewed the country's landscape for economic activities and found a growth sector and emerging sector in the banking industry in Nigeria. At this time the Nigerian banking sector was just coming into its own. Government-led reforms were repositioning it for growth, and a new crop of professionals was jumping into the fray—urbane visionaries with organizational and marketing flair. The income was below oil and gas industry standards, but it was a lot higher than my US$7 monthly salary. The sector also offered significant training, capacity development, and career progression opportunities. I was restless to get involved. So in 1998 I took the plunge and joined Guaranty Trust Bank (GTBank), an elite financial institution founded by Fola Adeola and Tayo Aderinokun, a couple of pioneering professional entrepreneurs and bankers. It was just as I expected it to be: frenzied, demanding, and results oriented. Banking suited my surging spirit, and I took to it quite well, moving from GTBank to Lead Bank and then Bond Bank, all in the space of five years. Still, I was restless.

In 2003 I quit banking altogether, took a chance, and struck out on my own, setting up my first private investment practice. As far as calculated moves go, this was a risky one. I had a young family depending on me, and I was abandoning a considerable level of comfort for the unknown. Well, the results were disastrous. I failed woefully and lost all the money we'd invested in starting up. It was a huge blow that knocked me a step back. But I had become quite acquainted with failing by that point in my life (with two failed businesses from my younger days and other failed attempts at achieving my goals), so I knew this was just the beginning of something bigger, and what seemed like a frightening reality at the time was subject to interpretation. This failing was part of the process and not the opposite. I was frazzled but unfazed. Nearing bankruptcy, I rerouted and plotted my dots in a different direction.

I took a job with African Capital Alliance, an investment firm headed by the brilliant Okechukwu Enelamah, who would go on to become minister of industry, trade, and investment under President Buhari's administration in Nigeria. Why did I take another job, having just quit one to start my first investment firm? I realized my financial skills and track record were mostly around structuring, raising, and deploying debt capital. I had neither limited practical experience nor a track record in equities, whether private or public. In a market where there was a significant number of people with similar debt capital skills, I offered nothing unique. I was basically offering a commoditized product where there were many alternatives, and the customer dictated the terms. Plus, there were other firms already established and well known in the debt advisory business.

I decided to skill up where I was weak (and shockingly, most people were too): equity capital structuring, fundraising, and deployment. I reasoned that Nigeria was going through a transition; the newly elected democratic government was opening up the country, implementing policies that would spur economic diversification, such as the deregulation of key sectors. New businesses were being formed. International interest in the country was growing. Partnerships, collaborations, and joint ventures were becoming more frequent. Equity capital seemed to be a strong and informed bet for me. Most people were still focused on debt capital, which to date still forms the largest pool of capital and talent in the financial industry in Nigeria and on the continent. African Capital Alliance was a new firm focused on private equity in Nigeria, and I spent the next four years there building wide-ranging equity investment and portfolio management experience across sectors.

Technology was establishing a foothold both in Nigeria and on the continent, and we were right there in the thick of it. The company's portfolio included leading companies, including MTN (the leading mobile telecommunications company in Africa now), GS Telecom (now Vodacom), and Resourcery Networks. I gained a lot of valuable experience working with great minds at the firm and leading entrepreneurs of the portfolio companies. I learned new ways of doing things and built an enormous amount of goodwill and a valuable network of colleagues, collaborators, and partners. My time at African Capital Alliance prepared me for the journey ahead in no small way.

So in December 2006, when I made the decision to launch out again, I was prepared. In 2007 I started Synergy Capital, an investment and advisory firm. Synergy Capital would grow to become a household name in private equity in both Nigeria and Africa, and it remained so until I left in 2019 to focus on the next phase of my life. The seeds I sowed throughout all those years from NNPC to Synergy Capital grew to become what is today Platform Capital.

My journey has since turned out to be one of creating impact, mentoring, philanthropy, and teaching, and the twenty-five years I worked in engineering, investment banking, and private equity are the dots that connected me to it. If I didn't embrace my failings, if I had allowed my setbacks to becloud me, or if I did not demonstrate the courage needed to take definite steps in pursuit of the dreams the universe had placed in my heart, the picture would have looked very different.

Success is a journey with several stops and milestones, and each of them is the sum of all our decisions and actions, our failings and wins, our rejections and acceptances, our criticisms and endorsements. And as your journey is unique, so will your milestones be different, with different variables leading you to different paths. What worked previously may no longer apply. So your journey requires conscious appraisals and compass checks. Anchor the chances you take in authentic values that guide you and build character. Discover the tools you need for each stage of your journey: What new skill? What stronger habit? What relationship? Whatever tool you do not have, acquire and learn to master with use. Each new level will bring a fresh set of challenges, and you have to be in a constant state of scenario planning, of anticipating the bumps and curveballs life will throw your way. One thing is certain: it will be a bumpy ride.

But there will also be smooth patches and wins and validating experiences. Do not let those deter you either. Focus on your journey and your goals. Keep evolving. Keep growing. Keep learning. You are a work in progress. You are still in play. To live is to strive forward. There is always something ahead you want and need and are reaching for. To get there you will also need to be brutally honest with yourself. No one knows you as well as you know yourself, so no one can do this for you as effectively as you can for yourself. By having a "work in progress" mentality and knowing

> The size of your ambition positively correlates with the pain you will experience.

you are not the finished product yet, by being necessarily critical of yourself, and by staying focused on your journey, you position yourself to take the hits you are sure to get along the way. Also know that the size of your ambition positively correlates with the pain you will experience. Huge ambitions require commensurate levels of sacrifice and guarantee different dimensions of pain when things go wrong.

History is replete with stories of successful people who blazed trails and pioneered great things. But the color of success often shades the shadows of failure and pain. So consider your journey. Do not obsess about things such as what your purpose is or what path you should be on. Remember, you create paths that are only visible in retrospect by taking chances, by stabbing forward, by following the voice in your heart, and by ignoring naysayers.

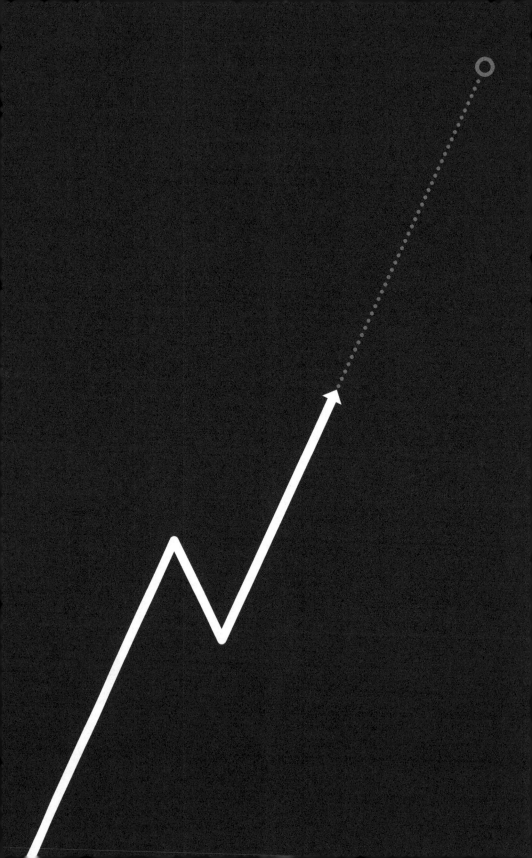

CHAPTER FOUR

(THE) BURDEN OF NAYSAYERS

· ·

Faith is the engine room of dreams. To drive a vision, you need conviction. Taking chances, laying dots, and pursuing an idea all require courage, and courage is predicated on how much of your pursuit you believe in, on how much of yourself you trust. Winning requires radical self-belief—radical because faith and conviction are less prevalent in human nature than doubt and fear, which are evolutionary legacies inherited from our ancestors, who needed heavy doses of caution to survive the predators that stalked them and the harsh conditions of their time. To thrive in today's world of high-speed change and uncertainty, we must work in the reverse.

Fortune favors those bold enough to heed the relentless calls of the visions in their heads. Manifesting a dream is akin to magic. It is translating the abstract into the tangible, the unseen into the seen. It is taking the absurd notion of human flight and forming it into an airplane. It takes a sharp shift in logic to believe in magic because we have been trained to trust what we see and *only* what we see. And because dreams are often private matters of the individual imagination, they are likely to be met with naysayers. People will say it cannot be done because it has not been done before. Other people will say it can be done, just not by you because, as far as they can see, you do not possess the resources that qualify you. It is hard enough to confront your own doubts, and it's harder still when they are reinforced by others. This is what makes conviction a revolutionary act and a prerequisite for realizing the magic of dreams.

The "miracle" of human flight was the manifest vision of two bicycle salesmen from Dayton, Ohio, who had no college education, money, or influence. Wilbur and Orville Wright were the sons of a preacher and a dressmaker. What they lacked in formal technical training they made up for in aggressive curiosity and daring. According to Orville, "The greatest thing in our favor was growing up in a family where there was always much encouragement to intellectual curiosity. If my father had not been the kind who encouraged his children to pursue intellectual interests without any thought of profit, our early curiosity about flying would have been nipped too early to bear fruit."

On December 17, 1903, near Kitty Hawk, North Carolina, Wilbur and Orville—having invented their own engineering process—made history by embarking on the first powered flight on their homemade plane. It was a torturous journey fraught with numerous failed attempts, endless revisions, and vociferous naysayers. And it was not until September 1908 that they were taken seriously.

Reports that the brothers had been working on a flying machine heavier than air had been met with great skepticism. In fact, one of the leading scientists of the time, Simon Newcomb, had put forth seemingly irrefutable logic demonstrating the impossibility of flight.

On October 22, 1903, less than two months before the Wright brothers' first flight demonstration, Newcomb published an article insisting that flying was impractical nonsense, and if it indeed were to happen, it would be met with a disastrous fate. He wrote, "Once he slackens his speed, down he begins to fall. Once he stops, he falls a dead mass. How shall he reach the ground without destroying his delicate machinery? I do not think that even the most imaginative inventor has yet even put on paper a demonstrative, successful way of meeting this difficulty."

Newcomb was not the only skeptic. Newspaper reporters who had gathered to witness one or two not very successful demonstrations by the brothers stopped coming altogether. Asked why the newshounds had ceased to attend, Dan Kumler, city editor of *Dayton Daily News* at the time, replied, "We just didn't believe it." Alexander Graham Bell, celebrated scientist and inventor of the telephone, published a statement in 1907 expressing concern about the reported speed of the Wright brothers' machine, concluding it was too dangerous and impractical to be sustained. In 1905 the brothers had written to the secretary of war at the United States War Department, seeking to give the United States government the first opportunity to control all rights to their invention. They received an irritated and terse reply in response. The Board of Ordnance and Fortification did not care to take any further action until "a machine is produced which by actual operation is shown to be able to produce horizontal flight and to carry an operator." Wilbur and Orville, holding on to their idea with strong conviction, were more amused than angry. They kept at it, and on September 3, 1908, five years after their first demonstration, at a formal public demonstration of flying at Fort Myer, all doubts disappeared.

Even then, fewer than one thousand people had shown up for the highly publicized event, expecting it to end in disaster. Theodore

Roosevelt Jr., who had come to witness the happening on behalf of his father, described the event as follows: "When the plane first rose, the crowd's gasp of astonishment was not alone at the wonder of it, but because it was so unexpected. I'll never forget the impression the sound from the crowd made on me. It was a sound of complete surprise." When Orville Wright landed the plane, he was astonished to be greeted by three or four newspapermen eager to interview him, each with tears streaming down his cheeks.

Chasing a dream is a lonely journey and one we embark upon to a chorus of opinions: family and friends who barely understand what we are trying to accomplish but love us anyway and want to see us win, experts in the field who think our attempts at something different are illogical and misguided, investors who take a hard pass because they "just don't see it," adversaries who take pleasure in our setbacks, timid minds who know neither the joy of victory nor the burden of failing but nevertheless draw their self-esteem from the failure and struggles of others, indifferent observers who are curious to see the outcome and quick to make your mistakes a platform for analyses. All of these are constants. The higher constant, however, is your opinion. The opinion that matters most is *yours*. When the chips are down, you bear the final burden of failing and the deepest joys of success. So it matters most what you think. Whether you are starting a business, launching an endeavor, choosing a course of study, building a career, or starting a family, the first naysayer to ignore is yourself.

There is no one more acquainted with your failings and your flaws than you are. You live with them. The memories and traumas of every misstep you have made, big and small, are in you and with you. No matter how many external cheerleaders you have, if the nagging voice of

> The first naysayer to ignore is yourself.

doubt within is louder and more persistent, it will be nearly impossible to make meaningful progress. This is why a healthy perspective of failing is crucial to your life. Your past, present, and future mistakes do not define you. Your flaws, whatever they are, are not permanent markers that restrict how far you can or cannot go. You must look yourself in the mirror and accept what you see, warts and all, because without a healthy sense of self, you will be drowned in the inevitable negative feedback that will flow your way from people and life.

Evidence from behavioral science shows a relationship between our levels of self-acceptance and the volume of gray matter in the regions of our brain that control stress regulation, pride, and theory of mind. The more negatively we feel about ourselves, the less brain tissue we have to effectively process stress and deal with anxiety. In other words, poor self-acceptance disrupts our emotional control on a chemical level. Conversely, a higher self-esteem has been found to predict higher psychological well-being and lower reactivity to stressful events.

So practice self-acceptance as a matter of survival. Be compassionate with yourself. No matter how bad your circumstances are currently or have been in the past, and whatever role you think you have contributed to it, take a different perspective. What are the lessons? What are the opportunities? It is easier to forgive yourself when you realize that failure is not the negative occurrence you have been trained to believe it is but rather a gift, a signpost directing you toward surer paths of success. If you cannot accept yourself enough to believe in yourself, nobody else will believe in you.

We have spent many years investing in businesses and ideas, and to us, the people behind these businesses and ideas, the confidence they have in themselves and their ideas, are vitally important. No matter how powerful an idea is, if the people behind it will fold at the first sign of trouble, the dream is dead on arrival. And there will be trouble—lots of it. So you have to believe in yourself enough to possess the emotional bandwidth you need to deal with knocks as they come. It is important to state that self-acceptance does not preclude self-appraisal. In fact, being able to objectively evaluate yourself, knowing what your strengths and weaknesses are, is a key sign of self-acceptance. Failing is only as valuable as your ability to step back, take stock, draw lessons, and change direction without allowing any of that to affect the way you see yourself.

Effective self-reflection enables self-regulation and makes the pursuit of your dreams an intentional and viable act, an unstoppable motion unimpeded by any other person's opinion. As the Greeks famously carved into stone at the entrance to the Temple of Apollo over two millennia ago, "Know thyself." When you do, no contrary label will fit you. Self-knowledge is the fruit of your journey, one discovered through action, through the application of your ideas, through your relentless engagement with life, your failed attempts, and your responses to them. The yes within you must be stronger than every other suggestion to the contrary.

Two years after I started Synergy Capital, the 2008 global financial crisis struck. The world's biggest economies were sent into a tailspin, and the shock waves could be felt from Asia to Africa. We were just starting to get our feet wet, and along came a storm of an event. But we were hungry and ambitious. We saw an opportunity in the midst of the crisis to buy good assets at good value, and we were going to take it. To do this we needed to raise funds, a significant war chest that outstripped our capacity at the time. So we headed out and combed every local pension fund available ... with little success.

Accompanying us on our quest was Ibrahim Dikko, a close friend and trusted businessman. In 2012 still knocking on doors, Ibrahim introduced us to the pioneer CEO of FSDH, who in turn introduced us to Zachariah Mahmoud, owner of an investment firm in London, who then introduced us to J. P. Harrop, a fund administrator with Augentius, one of the largest independent private equity fund administrators in the world, who pointed us in the direction of Kuramo Capital Management.

I packed my bags and headed to New York. My initial attempts to sit down with Kuramo yielded no results, so I tried everywhere else. The responses were disheartening. My status as an outsider stood out like a sore thumb. People laughed at my accent. I had one unsuccessful meeting after another with zero responses to my proposals. I was told twice and thrice that our adventure was unfeasible.

Then I went back on the trail of Kuramo and stalked their offices. Every day in late fall/early winter in New York, I stood at the door of the imposing 500 Fifth Avenue building in Manhattan, hoping to catch a glimpse of the legendary investor Wale Adeosun, the founder and chief investment officer of Kuramo Capital Management. Days went by without a single sighting of the great investor. Then one day fortune smiled on me. I met a gentleman walking out of the building and took a chance on engaging him. It turned out he was interning at Kuramo. I threw my best pitch at him. The poor guy must have seen my desperation and will to survive, as he politely and professionally invited me into their office to meet the founder and cofounder of Kuramo Capital Management. I walked into that big multiwindowed office and was ushered into a glass boardroom with nowhere to hide. All the months of chasing and looking for an anchor investor had come down to this moment. Every emotion one can imagine suddenly turned me into their home.

I met Wale Adeosun and Shaka Kariuki, founding and cofounding partners at Kuramo Capital, and blurted out all I had on my mind, in my heart, and in my soul. Years later Wale said he saw my hunger and willingness to succeed fill up the whole room. While I did not get a commitment from Kuramo Capital Management that day, I got very useful feedback, tips, and pointers. Most importantly, I got a coach, mentor, and sponsor who taught me a lot about the private equity fund management business.

Over the next year, I learned a lot from Wale, and he was very generous with his time and knowledge. He has a calm, wise, and nurturing mind. Wale and the Kuramo Capital Management team were extremely influential in Synergy Capital's fundraising effort. They invested, introduced other investors, and advised us as we sought to navigate the fundraising terrain.

We exceeded our target for a first-time fund manager, raising over $100 million—a very rare feat by a team of "local boys" with no Ivy League education or association. It took all of the two years of people saying it could not be done. They weren't saying it because the money was not out there or the idea itself was outlandish but because they believed we did not have the capacity. We were punching far above our weight. As far as they could see, we did not have the right track record or associations. Maybe they were right, but we had enough self-knowledge to not allow the opinions of other people to affect our drive. We were deaf to naysayers then, and we're deaf to naysayers now.

Allow me to connect the dots: Ibrahim Dikko—a fine and distinguished banker, entrepreneur, and lawyer who started the chain that led to Synergy's fundraising success—is an entrepreneur I worked with years earlier at African Capital Alliance. The intern who took me into the Kuramo Capital office was Olamide Adeosun (Wale Adeosun's son), who is now an excellent investment professional in his own right. The dots do connect, but you must lay them first. Laying dots is about taking chances on people, time and again, without knowing whether doing so will pay off. But you will never know if you don't try, and dots are only connected from back to front. So take chances, lay your dots, believe in your goals, and don't let anyone tell you what you can or cannot do.

Before Kuramo Capital Management gave us a chance, I knocked on over a thousand doors, sent countless emails, and called more investors than I can count. The efforts birthed only undesired outcomes, not failure. I learned a thousand ways of not engaging investors. So by the time I finally met with Kuramo, I was ready— ready to learn, ready to run, ready to seize the moment. All the *nos* prepared me for the *yes*. I have gone on to raise several hundreds of millions of dollars with phenomenal accuracy and timing, positioned by the experience gained during that trying period. Indeed, the universe listens, and magic happens.

The story Toye just told is priceless. It essentially underscores the idea that you are the owner of your story, and no one can direct its plot better than you. Toye and I believe very strongly that when people tell you something can't be done, often, it is usually a strong indication that you are attempting something original and audacious. What is also quite humbling about Toye's Synergy Capital narrative is that, at the time it took place, Synergy Capital became only the third firm in Nigeria to have raised that kind of money. Could it have failed? Probably. In fact, there were times when it seemed like it was not going to happen. But those moments only produced feedback from the future and instruction to history, and that is what our actions or inaction will ever do.

I started out in consulting part time in 2000 and fully zeroed in on it by 2002. I was a creative rebel then; I am one till this very day, and I will be till the day I die. All human ideas are born with an expiration date, and it is the duty of a few good rebels to spot this date and disrupt the old with new thinking, fresh perspectives, and new experiences. As a proud iconoclast, I am one of the people with an unrepentant loyalty to the continuous replacement of prevailing ideas and beliefs regardless of who is standing with the old. So on many levels, I am self-taught with an incredible blend of gift, aptitude, and skill.

A mentor of mine told me that all that was not enough and that corporate Nigeria was not ready for me at the time. He said I would do better if I found a place with an established consulting firm, such as Accenture or a corporation of similar weight, where I could build goodwill and reputation capital to attract and keep the right clientele. I appreciated the counsel, but I despised that it was given to me. I was stunned by his loud confidence, ignorance, and assumption that I would do well only if I got a job and would fail woefully if I struck out on my own at the time.

Do note that, unbeknownst to him, he was echoing the words my late father delivered to me as I sat by his bedside in 1999, a few days before his passing. It's said that the final words of a man on his deathbed are destiny-sensitive instructions to be held as sacred. It was with unquestionable love, but deep ignorance, that my father was telling me that my chosen path of entrepreneurship was a waste of time and that I was not going to achieve anything or amount to any noticeable value. Very strongly and with much emotion, he made a passionate case for why a white-collar job was my redemption, considering all the years I had wasted struggling with all manner of vices. Now my father was no mean man, and his influence on me was rock solid. He delivered the oration at the burial ceremony of the great Nigerian icon Chief Obafemi Awolowo, so you can imagine his intellectual weight and how much he was revered, respected, and honored by his peers, mentors, and protégés. So his words to me in those long and torturous moments were indeed weighty.

Like I forgave my mentor, I forgave my dad instantly because I recognized the logic of his counsel, and I understood that truly, by the facts, his words were correct. Yet I was instantly deleting everything he was saying because the truth of my conscience and the faith in my spirit were positive intangibles beyond the limits of facts. My position failed the test of sense and logic, but it passed that of truth, audacity, and belief. Relatives and mentors (such as the one who advised me in 2002) are usually so blinded by the content of their own experiences that they stay true and loyal to what has worked and what is working and tend to forget that change is a constant.

I knew clearly enough to love these two important figures in my life but also to ignore their counsel and follow the passion of my soul to change the world. I needed to remain true to the path I was sure would lead to the successful future they desperately wanted me to have. As the legendary songbird Whitney Houston put it, "I decided long ago never to walk in anyone's shadow / If I fail, if I succeed, at least I'll live as I believe." I do not look forward to failing because it is uncomfortable and can be hard, but if I *am* failing, I do not want to blame any part of it on someone else.

Today my story is known. I have built a name and a brand. I am certain that almost all of the people reading this had never heard the name *Soriyan* before they came across my name. I suppose that illustrates how far off the mainstream grid my entire lineage was. The global value in the name has been amplified by my own losses and wins in the last fifty years of my existence, and I am still just starting out. God has permitted the universe to reward me with the opportunities to win consulting briefs at the highest level possible, beating some of the biggest names in the industry in the process. Today consulting represents less than 10 percent of the value I command. I have transcended it.

Failing is feedback from the future and instruction to history, *period*. Whether you are right or wrong, whether you are Akintoye Akindele or Olakunle Soriyan or anyone else out there, you are a slave of your own actions and forever so. What you must do may not even be a solid conviction, but if it is all you know to do, *do it*. To not act, for any reason whatsoever, will deny you the assurance of, at the very least, knowing if the idea was viable or, at best, failing; learning a different way to do it; and ultimately succeeding. Trust us, it is by far better than not acting at all. For if we do not act, results—favorable or unfavorable—will not exist, just regrets of what could have been. The gospel here is of clarity of self and clarity of purpose.

It is easier to be dissuaded when you are unsure of the specifics of your vision, but when no option exists on the table but inaction, the available must become the tried. The world today does not answer to vague and imprecise maneuvers, but it does answer to crude audacity. There are many times you will be clear about what to do, but there will be times when your next action will be premised not on knowing what to do but on knowing what *not* to do.

Uncertainty and the unknown are proofs of our frail humanity and cannot entirely be eliminated. You must understand the intricate threads that form the fabric of what you see so when people say it cannot be done, you have something to filter their opinions through. This *something* cannot be given to you or done for you. It is there in your spirit, a gift of nature, and it's certainly not a determinant of whether your decisions to act or not act are right or wrong, but it does mean you are in charge, and you own the outcome, whatever it is. It also makes it easier to analyze your failings and renavigate if things go in a direction other than the one you had intended.

THE ADVANTAGE OF CULTIVATING CO-TRAVELERS

It is easier to be confused by naysayers than it is to trust your inner counsel. But if you are clear and understand your *why*, then the required tenacity becomes easier to sustain. Your propelling ethos must be obvious to you and those intimate with your journey. The necessary counterpoint to ignoring naysayers is cultivating co-travelers whose spirits are a resounding support to your aspirations. It is harder, though not impossible, to go the required distance with only voices and circumstances that fuel your fear. Sometimes you need partners in destiny, faith to faith, people whose dreams answer to yours en route to your destination. But whatever the case, get going.

Sometimes destiny partners are not only people who believe in you but are also in partnership with your naysayers. They fuel you. They challenge you. They make you test your assumptions. Your doubters say you are wrong, so you can feel and taste what it's like to be right. As Kunle stated, the very fact that you have naysayers is proof that you have something going on worth taking another look at. Naysayers, for the most part, are people who have been trained to align with the status quo. Their ideas of success are derived from staying in line. So when they see you deviating, they are convinced you are on the wrong path.

> The very fact that you have naysayers is proof that you have something going on worth taking another look at.

Yet the laws of victory are contrarian. For you to be different from the norm, you must act in a different manner. The universe rewards you for your differences, not for your similarities. The universe only compensates anomalies. Almost everybody who has tried to do something different has faced criticism. People understand what they are familiar with, and they fear what they do not understand.

When the young mavericks who created Uber and Airbnb came up with these radical ideas circa 2008, they were met with stiff resistance from people who only understood the existing order. There was fear from taxi owners and deep concern from regulators. In fact, almost all of Silicon Valley's sharpest investors passed on Uber because it was so off the beaten path, and its chances of succeeding were quite difficult for them to envision. In June of 2010, the founders sent an email to 165 seasoned investors, pitching the idea. As many as 150 did not respond. One was so offended he unsubscribed from the mailing list. Most of the few who responded politely declined. Ron Conway, nicknamed the Godfather of Silicon Valley, an early investor in Google, Facebook, and Twitter—and a visionary in every respect—also passed. "This one looks like it's going to be a fight in every city," he remarked in an email to a fellow investor.

When the founders of Airbnb interviewed at the famous start-up accelerator Y Combinator, the hub's revered cofounder Paul Graham was incredulous. "People are actually doing this?" he asked, startled by the home-sharing concept he had just heard about. "Why? What is wrong with them?" Now these were all seasoned investors who were no strangers to innovation, but the ideas were so radically different they could not picture them. The reward for normal is normal. The reward for abnormal—well, we will let you figure that out.

When you throw a stone into the ocean, it creates ripples. You do not know how far the ripples go, and neither do you care. You just throw your stone. The same principle applies to taking initiative, investing in people, and birthing ideas. Just go for it. Plan, but do not overplan. There is no such thing as a *perfect* plan. Nothing is truly known until it is tested. As Mike Tyson famously put it, "Every fighter has a game plan until they get punched in the face." The magic is in starting. Setting your plans in motion is tough, but we are testaments to the possibility of birthing a whole new world if you believe in it, believe in yourself, and put in the necessary work. So stay positive and avoid negativity and the people who peddle it.

Mind your own business. Listen to feedback—encourage it even. But trust your instincts above all. Sometimes a proposition is so way ahead of its time that people who live in the now may have trouble picturing it. It is your duty to envision it, believe in it, and see it through. The destination is overrated. Focus on your journey and your experiences along the way. The only guarantee you'll get there is to keep going. So keep going.

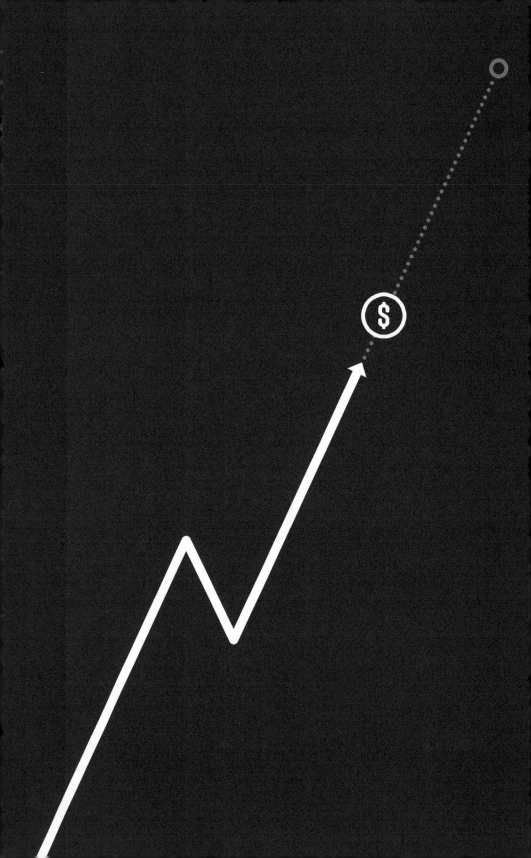

CHAPTER FIVE

THE COST OF VICTORY

· ·

Succeeding is an intentional act. It's a series of deliberate actions in the direction of your dreams and even more deliberate responses to the positive and negative feedback life throws at you. Intentionality is the universal language of significant achievement. Nobody stumbles into greatness. People who you think are successful because they are lucky are probably some of the hardest-working people out there. Yes, there is the unseen hand of grace, which we will speak about extensively in a subsequent chapter, but grace and fortune only meet you at a bus stop, and you will most likely have to crawl, cry, bleed, run, jump, and fall to

> Grace and fortune only meet you at a bus stop, and you will most likely have to crawl, cry, bleed, run, jump, and fall to get there.

get there. That is the cost of victory. The scale of your dreams and ambition directly correlates to the sacrifices you are willing to make and the level of work you are determined to put in. And perhaps the effort most likely to yield the best reward in executing your vision is the work of preparedness. If you take your time measuring before cutting, you cut clean. You measure twice; you cut once.

"On your mark, get set, go!" That phrase signals the start of a much-awaited activity. It could be an activity with a ten-second life span, like a one-hundred-meter race, or it could be a marathon. Whichever the case, a "ready, set, go" is a call to witness the result of days, months, years, and lifetimes of preparation. It assumes every participant is prepared and ready. But are they?

People often confuse preparation with readiness, but they are totally different things. Preparation occurs in a controlled environment, while readiness takes place in the "real world," where events have no respect for your expectations and are not dictated by your preferences or prejudices. In other words, preparation depends on factors within your control (leveraging strengths, removing weaknesses, exploiting opportunities, and wiping out identified threats), while readiness involves confronting a slew of internal and external factors outside your direct influence. You can be prepared based on seemingly airtight plans and hypotheses and still be unready for what reality will bring. Yet you will never be ready if you do not prepare, and you will never know unless you try. No matter how well prepared you are, your readiness will only be tested and revealed by your journey.

What is coming will come; it is who you are, how you see, how you hear, how you interpret, how you judge, and how you act that make the difference. Preparation is a second-level activity in the fulfillment of a goal, the first being the identification, definition, and articulation of said goal. Preparation is extremely important and is the foundation upon which success and the attainment of your goals are built. Planning, equipping, conditioning (physical and mental), simulating scenarios, iterating, and backtesting are all very important tools of preparation.

However, there are four overlapping dimensions of preparation that get you ready for facing real-life challenges and exploiting failure effectively. They are physical preparedness, mental preparedness, emotional preparedness, and spiritual preparedness. A critical part of what Kunle and I share is the significant investments we make in ensuring these core elements are well aligned as we engage the series of tasks and activities in the direction of our goals. Your journey will test you along these lines: physical, mental, emotional, and spiritual.

PHYSICAL PREPAREDNESS

Whether you play sports or write software codes, your physical body is indispensable hardware that you will need to keep in the best of shape. It must be optimized to bear the weight of your vision and the demands of the typically arduous road en route to it. Without the body, no motion is possible. In the hustle-prone state of our fast-paced postmodern existence, the body is most often ignored until it breaks down and halts everything with it. You have to be alive to execute the content of your existence, whatever it is. So you cannot afford to play with your health. Your body may not feature prominently on your balance sheet, but it is the strongest asset in your possession. Everything else you lose can be replaced except you. So exercise and eat clean. Get checked up regularly. Invest, as a matter of priority, in your health.

Physical preparedness also includes your appearance. How you show up and the impressions you create matter more than we like to admit. It sounds almost trite, but appearances are important. There's a multibillion-dollar industry in personal grooming and self-care that exists beyond vanity. Significant personal and business decisions are made almost every minute based on appearance. In fact, a 2009 study on the effect time spent grooming has on earnings demonstrates that taking care of your physical appearance is not so much the nonmarket activity we assume it to be, showing a correlation between personal grooming and increased levels of income. Sociologists tell us that the amount we groom ourselves communicates a significant amount of information about our desires, ambitions, and place in society. So control the narrative of what people think and say about you. Whether the intention is to stand out or blend in to achieve your goal(s), investing in your physical appearance (what you wear; how you walk, talk, look, and shake hands; etc.) is a key aspect of preparation, just as is investing in your health (exercise, medical checkups, vitamins, healthy diet, etc.).

MENTAL PREPAREDNESS

The body carries the mind—and the mind the body. Mental preparation is achieved by devoting significant effort and time to knowledge acquisition, competence building, and the improvement of resilience and focus. This is extremely important, as mental strength enables us to extract more from our body and other physical assets. Developing our mental capacity positions us to better anticipate and eliminate possible obstacles, understand the competition where it exists, conceive of well-thought-out backup plans, and map out strategies, all of which come into play in building sustainably for all that is ahead.

In addition, resilience, focus, and recognition of the dynamic nature of reality to discern which strategy or game plan is optimal are also critical on the journey. It is hard to find any successful person, regardless of specialty, who has not mastered this. This includes pivoting—knowing when and how to change course when things are not going as planned.

Twitter, the notoriously famous social media platform, actually started as a podcasting platform called Odeo. It ran into trouble when Apple launched iTunes, and with its much deeper pockets and extensive capacity, iTunes edged Odeo out of the market and toward extinction. Employees were reportedly given two weeks to come up with new ideas that could salvage the company. Jack Dorsey, who would go on to become CEO of Twitter, suggested the idea of sharing one's status—what one is doing, thinking, or feeling—a potential global stream of consciousness. That suggestion, one of the most successful pivots in modern business history, became Twitter, with a net worth of more than $10 billion. Developing physical and mental strengths is much easier to understand and perhaps achieve, but the next two are quite elusive.

EMOTIONAL PREPAREDNESS

Emotions are a more complex and misunderstood terrain, but they play a strong role in shaping the decisions we make in life. We are creatures of feelings and passions, much of which is an interplay between our perceptions, expectations, actions, and reactions to our external environment. Because our emotions are often a response to external stimuli, it is helpful to be intentional in creating our desired environment and investing in our emotional capital. This requires identifying the people who are related to your success and nurturing those relationships. You will need a lot of positive reinforcement along the way. A 2019 Wharton School of the University of Pennsylvania and City, University of London study examining the influence of group fear and group hope in decision-making determined that group "hope trumps fear." In other words, "the relationship between group hope and escalating commitment to a failing venture is stronger than the relationship between group fear and terminating that venture."

Surrounding yourself with people who believe in your journey gives you access to a brain trust, as well as emotional support when the going gets tough. We must, however, note that making this kind of emotional investment takes time and dedication. We usually do not see the need for it until that need is upon us. Speak to anyone who is successful at anything, and they will tell you the role that an investment in

> Grow your emotional capital by investing in valuable relationships.

people and relationships played in their success. From advising and helping you prepare for the road ahead to holding your hand and helping you cross your barriers, from standing in for you when everyone has deserted you to helping you get back on track when you feel like quitting, emotional assets and resources help create winners. Author and triathlete Baylor Barbee wrote, "When my body gets tired, my mind says, 'This is where winners are made.' When my mind gets tired, my heart says, 'This is where champions are made.'" The heart is about affection, and affection requires someone other than self. So grow your emotional capital by investing in valuable relationships. This will help nurture your emotional strength, which you can effectively draw upon when your body is about to give up and your mind is tired.

SPIRITUAL PREPAREDNESS

It is important to separate spiritual preparedness from religion or a belief in God or any form of deity, all of which are legitimate expressions toward the metaphysical component of the universe, which most people agree exists. Spirituality is about connectedness. The more spiritual you become, the more relatable you become. Connectedness with people, places, experiences, seasons, and energies is the character of spirituality at any level. Regardless of how we perceive it or the language we use to express it—call it luck, fortune, or serendipity—the universe reveals it now and again. Irrespective of your doctrinal history, the universe returns the energy you give it, positive or negative.

A happy person is more likely positioned to achieve his or her goals than an unhappy one. To invest in activities that make you happy is wise. Pursue what gives you peace. Strive to attain extended states of relaxation. Connect to your soul and purpose. Invest in family, charity, philanthropy, faith in God, reading, traveling, talking, and even silence. You have no energy for distraction and do not surrender to the common opinion that play is unserious. Play is focused rejuvenation when it's balanced with serious exchange. Work hard. Play hard.

Invest your time along this spectrum, and you will reap bountifully. This is soul renewal, a key factor in being successful and remaining a champion. Why do you have that vision or goal? What will you do when you achieve it? Knowing where you are going and why you want to go there will help you stay on track when everything looks bleak, when naysayers have written you off, when you have been laughed at, when family and friends have betrayed you, and when success does not look possible. God, the universe, whatever benevolent force you believe in is in your corner, guiding you toward an open door. Spiritual strength is what you draw on when nothing makes sense. Some people may question your sanity. Even *you* may question it at times, but your vision, goal, or target was revealed to you for a reason. Go for it with optimism and faith. Nourish your soul and spirituality. They come in handy when all else fails.

BEING READY

Readiness is a third-level activity, and it is at the center of executing your vision. How do you know you are ready? You do not. You never do. You think or believe you are, but you cannot be sure. For if you are ready, everything will go according to plan. As a Chinese proverb famously notes, "When the student is ready, the teacher shall appear."

But if there is one thing we can say about life, it is that curveballs are a real thing, and sometimes you will not see them coming. Assumptions are incorrect. People change. Realities evolve. While planning is a strategic activity, readiness is a more tactical but dynamic practice. It is the ultimate test of execution and vision. This is where champions become legends and where the mental, physical, emotional, and spiritual combine to chart big numbers for a sustained period. The trick to being ready is in investing time in the following:

- **PILOTING:** Take baby steps to understand the fast-evolving and dynamic reality you are facing.

- **BEING PREPARED FOR ANYTHING AND EVERYTHING:** Have a process in place that helps you appraise, iterate, synthesize, and adapt.

- ➡ **STAYING AUTHENTIC:** Know yourself, what you are capable of, and why you are on your chosen path.

- ➡ **PERSISTING:** Remember, stumbling is not falling, under is not over, buried is not dead, failing is not failure, delayed is not denied, and—most importantly—it is *your* journey, *your* story, *your* stage, *your* music, *your* play. Keep going.

Being ready is a tough thing to get used to. Through my transitions from an engineer to a banker and investor, from a son to a father, from a student to a teacher, from an entrepreneur to an "investpreneur," and—most importantly—from a man to a human being, I have always looked forward to the magic in each new stage and jumped at the chance to evolve. I view myself as a journeyman, a hope merchant, a bridge builder, a stargazer, a flawed and constantly evolving shepherd, and an incurable believer in the good in people and in their abilities.

When we launched our global platform, Unicorn Group, some years ago, we flew in over twenty African entrepreneurs, policy makers, and educators to meet Silicon Valley peers, investors, service providers, and leaders. Over the course of three days, we had about three hundred investors, entrepreneurs, and advisors come through to meet our African delegation. The interactions were robust, genuine, and value-centric. Partnerships and projects were created. The quality of the interactions, presentations, insights, and feedback were extremely beneficial to all.

At Unicorn Group we identify entrepreneurs and business models that are positioned to be winners and nurture their evolution and growth by providing more than capital. We enhance their ideation process by putting them in an ecosystem where they can access the latest information, tools, and skills while developing strong industry networks. This platform enables us to turn local ideas into global products, as we have the same infrastructure and facilities that we have developed in Silicon Valley in Mexico, Nairobi, Accra, Dallas, Johannesburg, Kampala, and Lagos. In addition, we are poised to open similar platforms in Marrakesh, Cairo, Shanghai, and Delhi. Our program ensures that our entrepreneurs are "glocal," that is, locally developing solutions that meet global needs.

All the entrepreneurs we flew to Silicon Valley experienced very important validations of their visions, received robust feedback on the potential of their products, had access to a universe of opportunity from their Silicon Valley peers, and attracted significant investor interest. It was a unanimously life-changing experience whose success had its roots in the discipline, dedication, and excellent delivery of the teams at Unicorn. These teams worked tirelessly to prepare, pilot, and execute plans that led to the continuing success of Africa House around the world, partnering with Eshirya Africa.

Since then, we have impacted and incubated over one thousand businesses and directly invested in over fifty within two years of that trip to Silicon Valley. We have partnered with global investment firms, universities, and international development institutions. Our vision of impacting one hundred thousand entrepreneurs and innovators over a ten-year period is enhanced by the quality of our partnerships, our continuous improvement, and our attention to feedback received. It is a heartfelt example of how extensive planning and preparation enable the sort of readiness we need to execute the robust desires of our hearts, a loose metaphor of what it is to win a competition, build a business, win a war, or whatever your goal is. By picking the right partners, agreeing on a vision, leveraging one another's strengths, appraising resources objectively (especially people), making decisions online in real time, and maintaining resilience, focus, and determination during challenging situations, success is inevitable.

Preparation gives birth to readiness, and readiness is what you need to turn even the most challenging scenarios and failures into stepping-stones for your next level. Life has rules that transcend geography and demography. You must understand them and work around them to get to your destination. No shortcuts, no windfall— the output is based on the input. Staying your course will lead you to your destination. Remember, being successful is not a destination but a journey, and it is *your* journey. Your view of success and your understanding of it must be yours and yours alone. It is simplistic to define *success* strictly in material terms. Being successful and being rich are not the same thing. Money is important, and we tend to think that if we do the right thing, money will come, but success and money are not the same thing.

Mother Teresa was a hugely successful human being. Was she rich? Maybe not in the material terms we understand. But she had so much goodwill from a consistent life of service that she could command and redirect material resources toward the causes dear to her. Define what success means to you. Understand the peculiarities of your journey. Then marry your journey and what success means to you and get to work. If things go wrong, embrace it as nature nudging you to take a detour. If things go right, then that is a usable thumbs-up. Keep going.

Listen to opinions, analyze feedback, process criticism, and put it all in context. Then after reviewing and contextualizing, in view of your plans, make the decision on what to change or do differently, if anything. Be bold enough to pivot if need be and determined enough to keep going if the path leads you forward. Just never give up or let anyone deter you. Never let anyone tell you what to want or justify why you want it. Persevere and watch that "lucky" break occur. The thing about lucky breaks is that they are not time dependent. The universe recognizes that your passion, commitment, willingness, dedication, and hunger will overcome any obstacle it sends your way, and it will give in upon your insistence.

We are passionate about being able to create a playbook and a narrative, particularly for the future generations of Africans across the continent and the diaspora, so they know that taking a chance on their dreams is a real possibility and that failing is not the end of the world. Do not be afraid to dream. Do not be afraid to fail. Do not be afraid of trying. Instead, be afraid of *not* trying because you never know at what bus stop grace will be waiting for you.

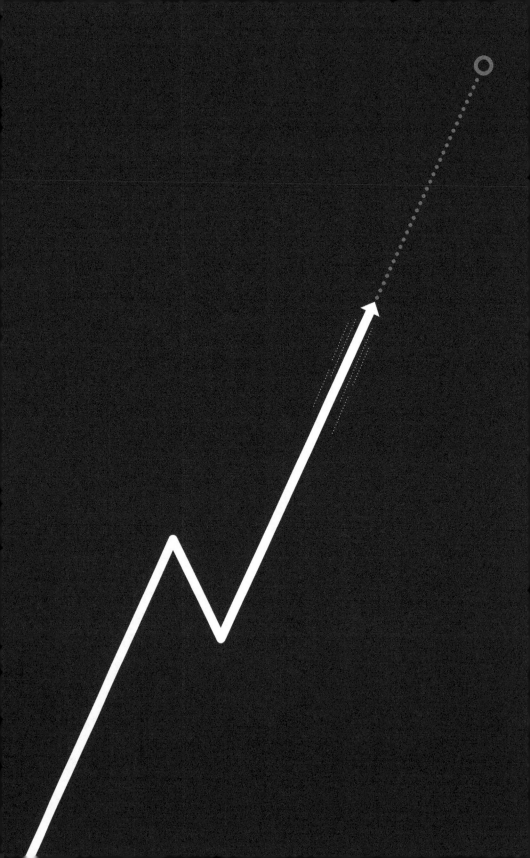

CHAPTER SIX

MOTION IS SURVIVAL; STASIS IS DEATH

· ·

It takes great vision to build a company like Kodak. Founded by George Eastman and Henry A. Strong in 1892, the company's radical entrance into the filming industry was a game changer on many levels. At a time when cameras were the preserve of large companies that deployed them for recording movies, Kodak democratized the human need for storytelling, memory making, and archiving by putting portable and affordable cameras in the hands of everyday people and households. The idea became a big hit, and the company name became synonymous with some of the most beautiful moments of our lives, so much so that we called them "Kodak moments."

By the early twentieth century, Kodak had cornered 90 percent of the photographic film market. Professional and amateur photographers relied on it. It grew its staff strength to 140,000 people, and in 1996, it was ranked by Interbrand as the world's fourth most valuable brand. But by 2012 this game-changing company, overrun by waves and waves of digital innovation, eventually filed for bankruptcy, becoming a cautionary tale for the business cliché "Innovate or die."

What we find particularly curious in understanding the decline in significance of such a huge company as Kodak is not just that it failed to effectively respond to the rise of digital photography in the late 1980s but also that the first digital camera was actually invented by a Kodak engineer, Steven Sasson, in 1975. The company was so afraid of what this product meant for the world of analog photography it had conquered that they practically buried it. For a company birthed by innovation, failure, and risk-taking, they were so comfortable with the status quo, so risk averse, they could not recognize the future even though they'd baked it in their own kitchen and held it in their hands.

The only way continuous success is guaranteed is by continuous failing. To have new successes, you must risk new failures. We have stressed that success is not a destination but a journey through the tunnels and toward broad horizons of life. What we must emphasize is that the complicated routes of failure that bring you to different stages of success in your life are similar to the ones you must take to keep progressing, and stagnancy is not an option. Gravity only pulls you down when you stop flying.

What we have discovered is that in almost every facet of life, when people become successful, they no longer want to endure whatever difficulties they went through that led them to the point of success. So they play it safe, stop dreaming, quit trying, and become unprepared for the inevitability of change. Life is a force that is constantly moving. It will come at you one way or the other. If it meets you in motion, it cushions the effect; if it meets you in stasis, it bowls you over. A life of continuing success demands ambidexterity, the ability to efficiently manage today's wins while probing for new pathways into the future. In other words, the true posture of success is Janus-faced, like the ancient Roman god of endings and beginnings, with one eye on yesterday and the other on tomorrow. This is something that must be understood and embraced on an individual level and at the corporate level.

One of the hardest things to do in life is to examine something that is obviously working and ask questions like, "Can it be doing better?" and "Can it even exist in another format, one completely different from its current one?" To question progress or success is an unpopular task, yet continuous relevance at the highest level demands it. Successful innovations and disruptions are known today only because human minds dared to question success and demand more of it. It is easier to focus on nurturing what is working than it is to pursue new directions of uncertainty. We call it the "foolishness of living with purpose" because a part of popular logic and intelligence must be jettisoned to find the inadequacies in what is already perceived as excellent and to birth something new and better from it. Human ideas cannot exist in perfection, and their imperfections present unique opportunities for innovation.

> Successful innovations and disruptions are known today only because human minds dared to question success and demand more of it.

It is important to recognize that you did not get to where you are now by doing what was easy. Today's competitive advantage, no matter how deeply heeled, will eventually succumb to changing trends. It is naive to assign permanence to what is obviously transient. It is pretty much the same as building your house on rented land. Look at history: The once formidable typewriter has given way to the personal computer. Telephone booths and wireless landlines have been eclipsed by smartphones. Video-streaming services have overrun the once ubiquitous DVDs. The lines will continually shift. If you refuse to participate in these shifts simply because you want to hang on to the false comfort of the current success, then indeed those who are shifting ideas will eventually relegate you to the past. None of us can afford to just sit on our perceived success; we have to keep going, keep trying new things. Motion is survival. Stasis is death. Invest in motion.

MESSAGE FROM THE AMBIDEXTROUS COMPANY

Enter Renault. The French car company has been around for a long time. It was founded in 1898 by three brothers—Louis, Marcel, and Fernand Renault—and boy, what a bumpy ride was to come! The company made its first volume sale in 1905, the early Renault Type AG1 cars, which were used to establish a fleet of taxis and later used by the French military to transport troops during World War I. By 1907 a large percentage of London and Paris taxis had been built by Renault. They were the best-selling foreign brand in New York during 1907 and 1908. By 1909 Louis was the only brother left alive, with Marcel and Fernand having passed due to a car accident and an illness respectively.

Having survived World War I, Renault became embroiled in World War II after the Nazis captured France. In March 1932 its production plant was hit and destroyed by RAF bombers with heavy civilian casualties. It was quickly rebuilt, only to be bombed again by the Americans. After the war the company was accused of collaborating with the Germans, Louis was jailed, and the company was nationalized after his death. But again it survived and remained a competitive European brand.

By January 1985 after a string of losses, Renault brought in Georges Besse as chairman. Besse instituted a string of reforms that turned the company around in four years. He was then assassinated in 1989 by militant anarchists disgruntled with his reforms. In 1992 Louis Schweitzer took over as CEO of the floundering company, and it is perhaps this period that gives us a proper sense of the company's resilience.

Over the years Renault developed what one of its executives referred to as the "desire to adapt." Its goals were reassessed every two years, and a culture of dissent, experimentation, and probing for new ideas was established. Renault achieved an ambidextrous structure that allowed it to maintain efficiency in areas where it had succeeded and also allowed it to take new risks. It pursued a risky alliance with Nissan, acquiring a 36.8 percent stake in it, and invested heavily in zero-emissions transportation research. By 2017 the Renault-Nissan alliance controlled ten brands and was the world's leading plug-in electric vehicle manufacturer with about 450,000 employees, selling more than one in ten cars worldwide.

No matter how rough its journey had been, despite whatever successes it acquired, the company refused to stay still. It kept moving, it kept adapting, and it kept winning. You cannot afford to rest on your oars, as they say, as tempting as it may be. The truth is success is such a seductive proposition. Once you attain it, you become preoccupied with sustaining it, and for most people, the instinctive way to do this is by hedging their bets. They simply, at best, recycle the new status they have attained for the rest of their lives and, at worst, suffer a harsh decline. It is what psychologists call a status quo bias, a propensity for sticking with the status quo because the perceived disadvantages of leaving it loom larger than the advantages.

In one experiment carried out by Harvard University researcher Richard Zeckhauser and his colleague from Boston University,

William Samuelson, some subjects were given a hypothetical choice with no defined status quo, framed as follows:

> You are a serious reader of the financial pages but until recently have had few funds to invest. That is when you inherited a large sum of money from your great-uncle. You are considering different portfolios. Your choices are to invest in: a moderate-risk company, a high-risk company, treasury bills, municipal bonds.

Other subjects were given the same scenario but, this time, with one of the options defined as the status quo, framed as follows:

> You are a serious reader of the financial pages but until recently have had few funds to invest. That is when you inherited a portfolio of cash and securities from your great-uncle. A significant portion of this portfolio is invested in a moderate-risk company.

Many different scenarios were investigated, all using the same basic experimental design. Aggregating across all the different questions, Zeckhauser and Samuelson discovered that an alternative became significantly more popular with the subjects when it was designated as the status quo. In other words, a significant number of the people in the experiment were unwilling to consider an alternative investment, regardless of its prospects, once the option of an already existing, moderately successful investment was introduced. We find ourselves wedded to existing measures of success because to strike out for something bigger and better is to risk failure.

It must be emphasized that this is not just a problem faced by start-ups. Even the most battle-hardened businesspeople and creators, who have ascended the heights by daring great things, find themselves unwilling to take new risks, only to plateau, sometimes unconsciously, faster than they'd imagined they would. Nobel laureate Richard H. Thaler once asked twenty-two heads of magazines if they would accept a hypothetical fifty-fifty investment that would pay $2 million to their parent company if successful or lose $1 million otherwise. These were seasoned veterans. Only three said they would accept the investment. The majority of them were willing to leave all that value on the table for fear of losing half of it.

There is an ironic sense in which success makes us averse to risk-taking because, after all, you've already made so much happen by trying and failing, learning and trying again, so why repeat this frightening cycle when you can just hold on to what you already have? Well, the thing is you cannot hold on to what you have by actually holding on to what you have. You hold on to what you have by throwing it back out there. This concept is somewhat reminiscent of a passage from Luke 17:33: "Whoever wants to save his life will lose it, but whoever loses his life will preserve it." It is human to keep taking risks the size of one's ambitions. If you want to be small, take small risks. If you want to be big, take big risks. Your rewards will be commensurate with your vision of the future and the attempts you are willing to make to actualize it.

THE LIMIT CALLED RETIREMENT VERSUS THE FORCE OF ADVENTURE CAPITAL

For a lot of people, what is known as retirement is a useful tool for shielding their hidden distaste for work and celebrating a legitimate, long season of no work, no risk, and—despite it—happiness forevermore. They quit dreaming and working to finally settle into the "enough" they have successfully put into the future in the name of retirement benefits. Yet go from country to country—developed, developing, or underdeveloped—and look for happy and contented retirees. What you will find, at best, is that the majority of the retirees are dissatisfied with the government of the day and are maintaining a loud voice in the polity about how they should be treated better and more fairly for all they have put in, as justifiable as that may be.

In a study I (Kunle) conducted in 2010, the question I had was this: could it be that the expectation gap many retirees across the world are dealing with could have been easily closed by a commitment to pushing themselves further than where and when they stopped in the name of retirement (by pivoting into another level of expression as a commitment to the dreams of their heart)? We interviewed 2,500 retirees in five states of Nigeria—500 in each of the following locations: Lagos, Abuja, Rivers, Enugu, and Kano. A total of 87 percent of the respondents stated clearly that beyond retirement benefits and passive income from investments, there were ideas and dreams in their hearts they could have pursued upon retirement. Another 76 percent stated that they believed their retirement benefits would see them through their twilight years, despite the nudging deep in their souls that it might not and despite the truth that there were options they could have committed to were it not for the lure of mental comfort that the idea of retirement provided. An incredible 95 percent of respondents agreed that although they'd officially retired and would not need to work again, it took actually retiring for them to realize that they had continued to work in a harsher and more demanding way that they were not prepared for.

The light of your dreams should not dim as you grow older. In fact, the reverse should be the case. One study in *The Economics of Aging*, published by the University of Chicago Press, found that the productivity of salespeople at a large insurance company, measured by the value of contracts sold, increases with age. Another similar study was conducted using a large data set on production workers at a German car-manufacturing company over many years and measuring productivity by the absence of errors in a well-defined production process. It showed that while the number of small errors is larger among older workers, major errors are more frequent among younger ones, with the measure of the researcher's productivity quotient showing that older workers demonstrate higher productivity.

There is ample evidence to suggest that our most productive years arrive in what is typically considered the twilight of our lives . In 2010 Benjamin F. Jones, an American economist and professor at the Kellogg School of Management, Northwestern University, published a study titled "Age and Great Invention." Using data on Nobel Prize winners and great inventors,

> Our most productive years arrive in what is typically considered the twilight of our lives.

Jones argued that "great achievements in knowledge are produced by older innovators today than they were a century ago." The average age of a Nobel Prize winner is sixty-two. The average age of a CEO at a Fortune 500 company is sixty-three. The average age of popes is seventy-six. Some of the most groundbreaking work in research and economic output is being done by people in what we assume to be the later stages of their lives.

Age or success should not circumscribe the limit of your achievements. There is still more land to conquer, still more room for growth and learning, for discovery and reinvention. When Bill Gates took his hands off the reins at Microsoft, he did not retire to a mansion on a hill, though he could afford to, as he had made enough money and enough impact for two lifetimes. Instead, he transitioned into philanthropy and making an impact in the medical field. Jeff Bezos, with enough money to never again lift a finger in his life, is taking on new challenges in space technology. Julia Child, the much-loved American celebrity chef, was a media and advertising executive who discovered her love for cooking later in life and transformed what started as a hobby into a phenomenal career, becoming the first woman to be inducted into the Culinary Institute of America's Hall of Fame. She kept going until she died at ninety-one. Our mental posture as we grow older and become more successful must be "What's next?"

Katsushika Hokusai, the Japanese painter and one of the greatest artists of the modern age, was seventy-five when he said the following:

Nothing I did before the age of seventy was worthy of attention. At seventy-three, I began to grasp the structure of birds and beasts, insects and fish, and of the way plants grow. If I go on trying, I will surely understand them still better by the time I am eighty-six, so that by ninety, I will have penetrated to their essential nature. At one hundred, I may well have a positively divine understanding of them, while at one hundred thirty, forty, or more, I will have reached the stage where every dot and every stroke I paint will be alive.

Hokusai died at the age of eighty-eight and created his best works in the last decades of his life, including *The Great Wave off Kanagawa*. There are still infinite possibilities stretched ahead of you and more meaningful contributions to make.

We are perhaps the most educated, skilled, and knowledgeable generation to ever reach midlife. We're more equipped to make magic than the generations that came before us. So you cannot stop working. Take on a new challenge. Learn new things. Make new mistakes. Learn new approaches.

Learn from John B. Fenn, who in his seventies won the Nobel Prize for his research that focused on a new way to identify and map proteins, carbohydrates, DNA, and other large biological molecules. He was fifty when he joined the faculty at Yale—an age some might consider old by the standards of academia. At sixty-seven he was forced into semiretirement, a moderately successful scientist who otherwise should have been happy to fade away into relative obscurity. Given his age and whittled-down position at Yale, he lost access to a lab and technical assistants. By all indications it was time to stop. But Fenn was still full of dreams and ideas and ready to explore his "what's next?" period.

So he went ahead and published a paper on a new technique he called "electrospray ionization," turning droplets into a high-speed beam that allowed him to accurately measure the masses of large molecules and proteins. This turned out to be a scientific breakthrough and was swiftly adopted by labs everywhere. At this point Fenn moved from Yale to Virginia Commonwealth University, where he opened a new lab and continued to improve on his idea. His work would go on to transform our understanding of cells, with his new method making it possible for biologists to identify molecules in a matter of seconds instead of weeks, significantly improving the turnaround time on research for new drugs. Fenn earned a Nobel Prize in chemistry in 2002, years after it was suggested he retire.

Some of the biggest success stories of our time (we are not talking about people who simply made lots of money but rather people whose impact on the world has outlasted generations) are those who repeatedly tested the boundaries of their capabilities. They relentlessly probed the status quo and kept probing until the sum of their lives became the stuff of history books. Of course, not all of us will be a Shakespeare or a Tesla, but we can live our life in such a way that the people within our orbit will be enriched by every vestige of talent and dream and effort we possess at every stage of our life, right until the very end. We must never run out of what we call *adventure capital*—the responsibility for taking on the impossible, an unrepentant resolve to defy the odds and go after paths less traveled and territories uncharted.

The courage to pursue something that has never been done produces the energy to birth newness. The courage to go after something *you* have not done before also produces the energy to birth newness. Refuse to allow your known success of today impede the possibilities of tomorrow. Both progress and continuous relevance are slaves of adventure. We owe it to our highest dignity and greatest legacy to embrace this capital. Risk is a constant. Failing is a necessity. Tomorrow and all the meaning trapped in it are released as humans retain a commitment to never settle.

Most of you did not become successful by being conservative. You got where you are by *daring*—by daring new things, by daring new directions—and by curiosity and an openness to surprise. You sure have not seen it all. Nobody has. At best, the Maker of life only permits us to experience just as much as we go after. All we know is what we have studied, but much more exists in the universe that we are yet to apprehend or understand. Accepting to stay fresh is also accepting to stay excited about the possibilities ahead. Retain an infinite sense of wonder. Breath is proof that there is still more out there to conquer. If the universe, in all its splendor and grandeur despite its age, is still expanding, still growing, why do you think you have seen all there is to see or reached the limit of your vision?

Science has been consistent in its commitment to letting us know that retaining a sense of wonder does incredible things for our mental and physical health. Positive psychology researcher Jennifer Stellar, in a paper on the effect of positive emotions on inflammatory conditions, including heart disease and cancer, showed the effects on our physical health of keeping a sense of wonder. The study, which analyzed cheek swabs from two hundred healthy volunteers, assessed through questionnaires the negative and positive emotions the subjects felt in the previous month. Evaluating the results, Stellar and her team discovered that those who reported feeling more positive emotions showed less inflammatory markers and that those who reported emotions such as awe, wonder, and curiosity showed the strongest correlation. Reporting this, she noted the following:

> One reason is that proinflammatory cytokines encourage social withdrawal and reduce exploration, which would serve the adaptive purpose of helping an individual recover from injury or sickness.... [A]we is associated with curiosity and a desire to explore, suggesting antithetical behavioral responses to those found during inflammation.

We believe in the infinite potential of the human spirit to keep producing until the physical body expires. We are committed to keeping on going in spite of success, in spite of failing. We believe in the elastic capabilities of the human spirit to bounce back from the most difficult circumstances, to endure the inevitable turbulence of our individual and corporate journeys. We refuse to be contained by the successes we have experienced and refuse to recoil from the possibilities of what lies ahead and the circuitous challenges that will lead us there. We know too much of the multilayered nature of failure to not embrace it as par for the course for the boundless dreams we have allowed ourselves to carry. This is life as we know it. And what a joy it is indeed.

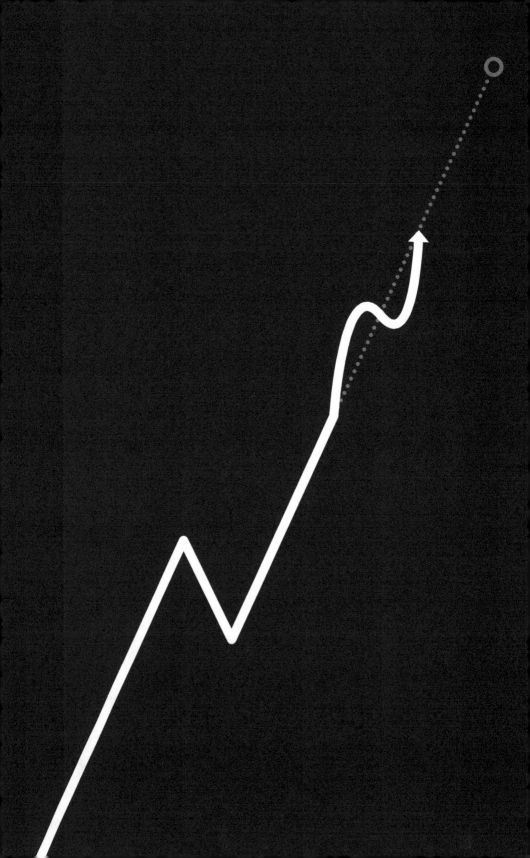

CHAPTER SEVEN

NAVIGATING TURBULENCE

. . . .

"Ladies and gentlemen, we are experiencing some turbulence; please return to your seats and fasten your seat belts." The plane, slicing through difficult weather, rattles on every side. For the pilot, the crew, and most seasoned fliers aboard the airplane, this is a familiar occurrence. They grit their teeth and ride it out. In fact, what any pilot will tell you is that turbulence is a perfectly normal experience when flying a plane. Most of them see it coming. Sometimes they avoid it so as not to unnerve the passengers; other times they just fly through it. Planes do not fall apart when they face turbulence. They are built to withstand it. This is akin to life.

Few things test our resolve like difficulty, and difficulty comes to all. Tough, turbulent moments make us want to take a step back permanently. They are hard to deal with because they contradict our expectations, turn the color of our dreams to black, and make us doubt ourselves and question our prospects. The truth is it is hard to keep going when you cannot see a way through, but just like every pilot knows, planes are built of stronger stuff than a few contrary winds—just like you are.

To assume that the difficult moments of your life are powerful enough to permanently derail you is to succumb to one of the trickiest illusions of all time. If you are reading this book, there is a significant chance that you have been through a difficult situation before. Think about how overwhelming and endless it felt at the time. Now think about how different the situation looks and feels in retrospect. The natural emotional response to a tough situation is fear and anxiety. But experience allows us to reframe and relabel.

A pilot flying for the first time and confronting turbulence, no matter what he or she has been told, is likely to experience some anxiety going through it. But facing it a second time and a third, he or she is able to see it for what it truly is, a temporary moment of discomfort. Some of these moments stretch out into longer periods than others, but all of them eventually pass. Scientifically, turbulence is incapable of crashing a modern plane. Save for a mechanical error of some kind, the plane ultimately gets to its destination. Passengers who experience severe turbulence on a flight often swear they'll never board another plane. Yet they do so again when a destination beckons. Your destination beckons. Fly toward it.

Abraham Lincoln is typically considered the poster boy of what a sagacious, empathetic, successful president looks like. The brooding orator held his country together through a vicious civil war and signed the Emancipation Proclamation. Yet Lincoln could very well also be the poster boy of hardship and difficulty. Born into rural frontier life in the early 1800s, Lincoln grew up poor. His mother, Nancy Hanks Lincoln, died when he was only nine years old. At seventeen he found work on a ferryboat and lived in a log cabin with his father. At twenty-one he built a flatboat and made a run down the river, moving to New

Salem, Illinois, in 1831. He got a job as a store clerk and set about making a name for himself.

His ability to read and write eloquently quickly set him apart in the largely illiterate town, and six months after his arrival, he announced his candidacy for a seat in the state legislature. He lost by a couple of hundred votes, turned briefly to business, and bought a store with a partner who died shortly after from too much drinking, leaving a flustered Abe with a hamstrung enterprise riddled with debt. He turned again to politics and was elected to the state legislature in 1834.

In 1838 Lincoln ran for the position of speaker and failed. In 1843 he sought nomination for Congress and failed. In 1846 he got elected to Congress. He sought reelection in 1848 and failed. In 1849 he applied for the position of land officer and got rejected. In 1854 he tried to get elected into the US Senate and was defeated. Two years later he sought the vice presidency and was rejected. He vied for the Senate again the following year and failed. In 1856 he ran for the highest political office in the land and won, becoming the sixteenth president of the United States of America. Lincoln's career as a politician was an unusual trajectory defined by relentless failing and difficulty but one steered by an equally relentless captain.

The difficult periods on the road to your destination are not markers signifying the end. They might give you a bit of pause and make you reevaluate your position, but if you hold steady, you will make it through. Another interesting thing about experiencing turbulence while on an airplane is that nobody on the ground, looking up, can see the plane shaking. Only those inside experience the discomfort. To paraphrase a Maya Angelou quote, "They see your glory, but they sure do not know your story"—an apt statement indeed.

It is interesting how people assume your life is amazing based on what they see perhaps on your social media platforms, the limited time they spend with you at social functions where you are looking your best, or the gossip they hear about you. No one truly has it smooth. No one ever has or ever will. Check your holy books. Consult your philosophy texts. Life was not designed for uninterrupted stretches of ease. There will be ups and downs. There will be turbulence. Your journey is and will be a bespoke ride of pain and pleasure, sweetness and bitterness, pleasant surprises and disappointments. You will have a lot more ordinary and bad days than good ones, days where you are scrapping and fighting to survive, days when you will consider packing up and running away, days when you cannot catch a break. Then there are the days when nothing good or bad happens—just plain, simple, regular days. So when the glory days come, enjoy them!

The universe and its Creator are reminding you that your existence is not forgotten. The universe rewards perseverance, dedication, and commitment. We are gladiators fighting in the Colosseum. Every day we fight beasts and humans alike for our survival. It is a "kill or be killed" game, and at the end of the day, at the end of the battle, you find yourself bloodied, tired, and weary. When you survive, the crowd cheers. Are they cheering your story? No, just the moment! Most times spectators are not even watching the fights. They are chatting, drinking, doing whatever, and when they hear the cheering, they join in mindlessly. It is you in there, out there, fighting for your life. You enjoy the cheering for a moment, knowing full well that you cannot let it get into your head because the loud cheers can quickly turn to boos and lead to your death. So you stay alert, focused on the battles ahead, hungry, and ready for anything. You will lose some fights, get hit, fall down, and get cut, but you stand and fight and make sure you win.

I am grateful for all the awards that have come to me in my long, checkered career and life, all of them. They are from my Creator. I accept the gifts the same way I accept the pain, the betrayals, the losses, and the disappointments. I accept them on behalf of my loved ones, partners, and friends who are there when no one is cheering. The awards are as much for them as they are for me. Without them, I am nothing.

I completely align with Toye's sentiment. We share some very bad days as well as good days with high energy, a crazy tempo, deep mental exchanges, and drums of happiness. This is usually what people see— young people especially. They set their imaginations loose, painting all kinds of scenarios about the ease of life and how they will do anything to live this one-sided life of happiness forever. They often miss the big picture.

Good days are the seasons the universe invests deep in your soul. They are elastic and transferable values you will need to pull from for the contrary seasons ahead of you. The demand of life is to deploy both the wisdom to celebrate the good days with visible gratitude and the courage to contain the bad days with unmistakable character. Good days or bad days, we must keep our composure and adequately represent the purpose, meaning, and power those around us and those following in our footsteps must rely on to help realize their dreams

> Life is fair in that its sting of both bliss and misery is shared by all.

and aspirations. Good days are great and must be savored because they are the cushioning energy for tomorrow's dark days. Yet if intelligently embraced, bad days are filled with usable clarity and the direction that births unprecedented breakthroughs. So love it or hate it, the human journey is all about highs and lows. Either way, life will present you with the choice to either be pitiful or powerful, on the bad days especially. One day you could be on the top of the world, and the next day, you could be at the bottom of the ocean. Life will favor you today and be a pain for me at that same time, and it could be a pain for you on the same day of my own good fortune. Life is fair in that its sting of both bliss and misery is shared by all.

So brace ourselves we must, seat belts tightly fastened as we fly through life's wide-open skies of possibilities. We have seen too many dreams cut short by difficulty. It wasn't the difficulties in and of themselves but because the drivers, facing understandably tough situations, cut their "losses" and moved on. This is particularly resonant for young African entrepreneurs and innovators who face incredible odds in their relentless attempts to build something noteworthy. They stumble due to fundraising challenges, their dreams deferred for longer than necessary because securing capital for daring ventures is a hill too steep to climb. Sometimes when they do manage to raise some capital, they trip over inarticulate government policies that are constantly changing and infrastructural bottlenecks they do not have the liquidity to overcome. For many of them, one failure is too much to stomach, so they throw in the towel and settle for something within the confines of ease and mediocrity. What this means is that we lose too many great ideas in the throes of difficulty, and so too many problems go unsolved. For every dream that perishes in the turbulence of our harsh African skies, the light grows dimmer. This is why the courage to keep going, even in the face of difficulty, is imperative. As the adage says, "Success is not final; failure is not fatal. It is the courage to continue that counts."

The story of Colonel Sanders is familiar in self-help lore for how much it exemplifies the capacity of the human spirit to surmount hardship. At forty years old, Sanders was the owner of a roadside café. He had been fired from several jobs, and his marriage had recently broken down. The café, located on the side of a major highway, was soon shut down after another highway was built, and Sanders lost all his customers. At sixty-five he found himself broke and desperate, so he took his chicken recipe on the road. Legend has it that he would cook his fried chicken on the spot for restaurant owners to convince them to sell it to their customers. The rest is history. His Kentucky Fried Chicken (KFC) global franchise has since become a thriving global enterprise, eclipsing his years of struggle.

Before her hugely successful Harry Potter series, J. K. Rowling was a divorced mother on welfare who was going to school and trying to write a novel in her spare time. Recalling this brutal period in her popular Harvard commencement address, she said the following:

> So why do I talk about the benefits of failure? Simply because failure meant a stripping away of the inessential. I stopped pretending to myself that I was anything other than what I was and began to direct all my energy into finishing the only work that mattered to me. Had I really succeeded at anything else, I might never have found the determination to succeed in the one arena I believed I truly belonged. I was set free, because my greatest fear had been realized, and I was still alive, and I still had a daughter whom I adored, and I had an old typewriter and a big idea. And so rock bottom became the solid foundation on which I rebuilt my life.

It is with great pride that we share the silver linings of our own continuing journey of failing with you. We have spent a good deal of time urging you to take risks, to dare greatly, to embrace failure. We do this with all sense of responsibility, vulnerability, and truth. The truth is that we faced, are facing, and will continue to face difficulties. And you will face difficulties too—lots of them. We've lost more times than we'd thought we could possibly bear. You will lose more times than you think you can bear. Partners will walk away. Investors will jump ship. You will get the product wrong. Your market entry strategy will fall flat. A stronger competitor will beat you to it. You will find yourself questioning everything you have believed, even yourself. You will make mistakes. Like almost every pilot, you will see turbulence ahead and drive right into it. All of these things matter, and none of it does—not as much as how you react when everything crumbles, not as much as what you learn when it does and how you use it.

Ever heard of Traf-O-Data? Probably not. It was a computerized microprocessor built by Bill Gates, his childhood friend Paul Allen, and a University of Washington electrical engineering student named Paul Gilbert. Its job was to analyze traffic data from the black rubber traffic counters that are placed on roads and create reports for traffic engineers. On the day of their big launch, the device failed to work, and the business failed before it started. Allen later shared the following with *Newsweek:* "I have made my share of business mistakes, but Traf-O-Data remains my favorite mistake because it confirmed to me that every failure contains the seeds of your next success. It bolstered my conviction that microprocessors would soon run the same programs as larger computers, but at a much lower cost."

> To understand your motivations, limitations, and strengths is to be truly resilient.

Perhaps the most critical thing we learn in moments of difficulty is what they teach us about ourselves. Hardships are portals of self-discovery. *You* are the most important element in your journey, not your parents—God bless their hearts—not your partners or investors.

You. It matters who you are. It matters why you want to succeed. To understand your motivations, limitations, and strengths is to be truly resilient. If money and comfort is what you truly want—and we are not saying this is bad in itself; money and comfort are important—but if they are *all* you truly want, difficulties will test and reveal you. We believe there is something more and greater for you out there.

Arianna Huffington, the hugely successful cofounder of the *Huffington Post* whose second book, by the way, was rejected by thirty-six publishers, put it this way: "I strongly believe that we are not put on this earth just to accumulate victories and trophies and avoid failures, but rather to be whittled and sandpapered down until what's left is who we truly are." And who you truly are is a fighter and a champion for the common good. This is why we are rooting for you. To root for you is to root for all the people out there who are trying to better themselves and make a difference, regardless of the setbacks they were born with or the challenges they are currently facing. To root for you is to root for Africa, to root for Nigeria.

In the last couple of decades, we have been unfortunate representations of hardship and struggle on an individual and collective level. But what has happened over the years and especially in recent times is that our struggles have birthed a generation forging futuristic cities out of the rubble one idea at a time. Think of Japan after the war. Some of its cities were almost completely wiped out in the devastation, Hiroshima and Nagasaki. Think of the self-belief and determination, the concerted and collaborative effort between government, the private sector, and the young people who dared to dream. It was a recovery so astonishing that the rest of the world referred to it as the "Japanese economic miracle." Ground zero is a perfect place for rebuilding.

This is why we are confident about the future prospects of Africa and Africans. This is why we write and dream and work and invest in the possibilities we see manifesting, from Lagos to Accra to Nairobi to Joburg to Lusaka and across the continent. Our difficulties do not define us. Your difficulties do not define you. The world in itself has been written off more times than we can count. The generation that faced the bubonic plague, the Black Death, thought it was the end. The generations that faced the First and Second World Wars, which claimed more than ninety-seven million lives combined, thought they were witnessing the end of the world. The Great Depression, the Cold War, the world on the brink of nuclear annihilation, the Great Recession, the COVID-19 pandemic, and the waves of dictatorships and civil wars that spread across postindependence Africa and the apocalyptic predictions in their wake we have survived. We are more resilient than we dare to give ourselves credit for. We will continue to survive. We'll continue to thrive and fly through turbulence and chaos with destinations of greater prospects in our sights. We will get there. You will get there. This is why we are betting on you.

Do not let the challenges of the present moment deter you. We have seen this movie before. You survived. We did too. So keep going and keep going strong. Reach out for help where you need to. Sit down and rest for a while if you need to. Take stock. Reassess. Learn about yourself. Understand your mistakes. But get up again and keep going.

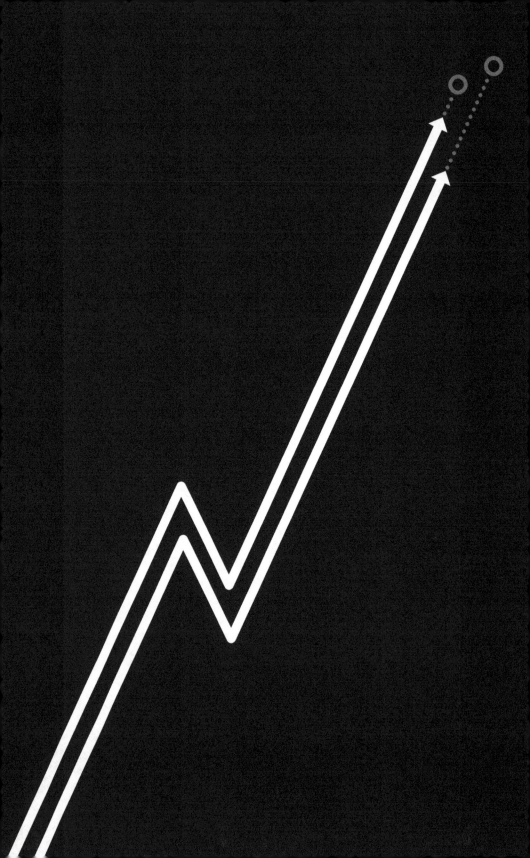

[CHAPTER EIGHT]

BE YOUR BROTHER'S KEEPER

. . . .

We have written extensively so far about the journey to a successful life; about the power of curiosity, taking chances, and embracing failure as a data point capable of guiding you into breakthroughs; about the need to be deaf to naysayers while you synthesize feedback; and about preparedness and readiness and the unseen hand of grace in the execution of your vision. But the question is, to what end? Why do you want to succeed? What does success mean to you? If the picture of success you have does not reveal what you will do with it, then you do not know what it means to be succeeding. Clarity is not simply being clear about your destination; it is more about knowing what you will do

> The purpose of success is to help other people become successful.

with what you attain when you attain it. In other words, your journey does not end with your becoming the best at what you have set your mind to; rather, it begins when you start doing something with it for others. It's simple: the purpose of success is to help other people become successful.

Viewed through this lens, it becomes clear that success is not a destination. You will never get to a place at which you have finally arrived and are successful. As long as there is one more person in need, one more person without, one more person who can use your help, then there is still work to do. Being our brother's keeper is something we take seriously because that is how we gauge whether we are succeeding or not. Our passing grade is not in the several material investments we have made successfully over the years. Our passing grade is in the hundreds of people whose school fees we are responsible for, the countless school fees we have paid locally and globally, and the over five thousand people we have fed every Friday over the past year. It's in the countless number of people we have supported with clarity and direction over the years. People sleep because we do not. Again we take this seriously.

They say investing in people is the most rewarding investment, and this is true. What we have is not ours to begin with. So we are not investing it per se; we're just giving people what God and the universe owe them, which we happen to be temporary custodians of and conduits for. Whatever we have or will have belongs to God and to the universe and will be left behind when we depart. Giving back and paying it forward is not an option or something we do because it makes us feel good. It is first a duty, then a lifestyle. It is why we wake up every day. It is why we work. We are nothing but unqualified shepherds, lucky to be able to help. What we have learned through years of striving and failing and learning and winning is that our principal job is to look out for others and God will look out for us. We must also emphasize our belief that there is something about all this that is innately African.

Community-based living and relationships have been an intricate part of the African value system since the period before colonialism, where individual identities did not exist in isolation but in relation to a community. As a people, our individual survival and prosperity were tied to the general health of the larger group. Our economies were sustained by communal farmlands and barns, trees and streams. Craftsmen and traders existed in cooperatives and healthy competition. Collective prosperity buoyed individual prosperity and vice versa. Poverty was not a mainstream phenomenon and was, where present, the result of a larger-scale climatic occurrence. Individual families in need did not find it difficult to ask for help. It was common to turn to your neighbor in your time of need, assured of relief. There was hardly a presence of roaming beggars without family or assistance, no motherless babies' homes or group homes for the elderly. The community pitched in across the board. We had communal squares and festivals, systems of beliefs that upheld morality and catered to the individual and collective psychological imagination within the boundaries of morality.

Even in the age of urban migration and modernity, where young people have taken to the cities in droves, there are still communal anchors, with extended families retaining cultural and sometimes economic influence, and people continue to return home seasonally for cultural events and activities. Remittances, which today constitute significant percentages of GDP, still come in from across the world. The Kenyan philosopher and writer John Mbiti put it quite clearly when he said, "In Africa, the individual can only say, "I am because we are, and since we are, therefore I am. This is a cardinal point in the understanding of the African view of man."

Postcolonial African experiences and the formation of nation-states across the continent have, however, seen a gradual erosion of this sense of community and its inherent advantages. Today one of the factors undermining our development as a continent and sustaining the sharp, frightening cases of inequality across Africa is the pursuit of private gain at the expense of public good, a trait that trickles down from political leadership and public office holders. The irony of it is that no nation-state anywhere in the world can survive without a sense of community and shared destiny. This is at the heart of the social contract, and until we rediscover it, the development we seek and pursue will continually elude us. Any claim to personal wealth in a society of widespread poverty and disillusionment is hollow at best. Therefore, as the authors of this book, we feel it is crucial we share our deeply rooted belief that nation building is a collective responsibility.

Nation building transcends the provision of infrastructure, such as roads, power, education, and healthcare systems. It is underpinned, more than anything, on the virtues of shared prosperity; of empathy, equity, and justice; of each one of us actively doing his or her part to make the lives of others better in whatever capacity we can. When we look out for one another, it enriches and connects us to people and ideas that positively impact our perspectives in life. It is critical that we invest in our largest asset: our people.

We need an educated, skilled, and literate workforce to build a diversified and resilient economy. We need an empowered entrepreneurial class to develop solutions, innovative business models, and new industries. We must invest in our women, who are the backbone of our societies and the stronghold of our families. Without them, we will never realize our full productive potential. We must also pay attention to every person's quality of life. Vulnerable social groups like abused women and rural children must have access to basic amenities and rights such as clean water and freedom of movement. We must make sure that everyone has access to quality healthcare. This is true now more than ever. If we do not take action as a collective across these five key areas, we cannot possibly eradicate poverty.

We believe that every citizen—business owner, parent, or young adult—has a role to play. We cannot rely solely on the government to provide public services. We must step up and do our part. Our world has made corporate social responsibility (CSR) very popular, but through each individual we influence, through each entrepreneur we impact, through every career we are privileged to advance, we try to hold them accountable to how they pass it on in an organized and scalable format. We call it PSR, personal social responsibility. This is the phrase to scale. We believe in the power of the village and its capacity to remind us of our duty and obligations to one another.

Growing up in the village, the whole community was responsible for the development of a child. Everyone participated in your education, development, and well-being. They encouraged you, celebrated you, and supported you. They chastised you when you strayed and collectively invested in your perception and view of life. Everyone was everyone's responsibility. This is the village architecture we seek to magnify.

In this rapidly evolving world, we believe now more than ever that empathy, togetherness, and collaboration are how we will create a better tomorrow. With our Village Ecosystem and Mindset Approach (VEAM), we aim to transform Africa by building a powerful village of local and global change makers. This type of community investing is crucial to the development of African countries. We have accepted that race, tribe, language, family, religion, and all other fences we have built around our lives are not real. We are all one under one sun and one God. The only way to unlock the potential of Africa is through an all-inclusive growth. All our human resources must be fully optimized for the journey ahead. We must leave no one behind. Everyone has a role to play in the Africa of our dreams and the Africa of the future.

Personally as authors of this material, we do not believe in saving in the traditional sense of keeping money in a financial institution. We believe that investing in people is the best way to save. To live a life worth living, you must give to others. Those who give to others live forever. That is true legacy. You cannot clench a fist to receive. No, you have to open your fingers and stretch your hands to receive. Everything you own becomes inconsequential to your individual existence when you die, of course, but when you give to the world, when you pay it forward, you leave a legacy of goodwill for those behind you that far outweighs any material possession you had or bequeathed to them. The best way to receive—and hence own—is to give.

If you save a hundred thousand dollars a day for ten years, you will not be a billionaire at the end of that period. If you continue saving for another ten years—making it twenty years in total—you still will not be a billionaire. For us, we would rather invest that money into our innovators, entrepreneurs, and communities; into ideas; into education; into healthcare. In ten years' time, one of those businesses could become a $1 billion enterprise, and even if it does not, the jobs we will have created, the families empowered, and the ripple effect on the overall economy and ecosystem will still be extremely significant.

Money is not supposed to be static. It is meant to be in motion, and the best vehicles to inject it into, as we have discovered, are people. You only own what you spend because everything you spend and spend wisely goes into the future to multiply. If you hold on to money, it leaves you. As the German reformer Martin Luther once put it, "I have tried to keep things in my hands and lost them all, but what I have given into God's hands I still possess." And how do we put into God's hands? By giving, contributing, and investing in others.

We concluded that three things happen to you when you give. One, when you give, and give extensively, it creates a need for replen-

CHAPTER EIGHT | BE YOUR BROTHER'S KEEPER

ishment. You have to employ your creative instincts to get more. You go hunting and gathering. Your skills and capacity for creating wealth are kept sharp. You become more competent. You become better. The summary is that giving increases your hunger and abilities for getting. Two, when you give, you are creating your own tomorrow and designing your own legacy. The quality of today is a result of yesterday's efforts. The outcome of tomorrow will depend on today's investments in others. Three, you create a community of givers. In a thousand years, the car we drove will not matter; neither will our bank statements or net worth. What will matter is the lives we touched and whom they touched in return.

The story of my life is that I am a child of grace. I grew up in southwest Nigeria with my father, Alhaji Akindele, who taught me the importance of grace, faith, and destiny. In his later years, we traveled a lot together, and from him I learned that we are nothing if our neighbors are nothing. This lesson has stuck with me over the years. It does not matter what you achieve or who you are. Being your brother's keeper and loving your neighbor is the

> We are nothing if our neighbors are nothing.

only way to have the life you desire and fulfill the purpose for which you were created. I believe my purpose in life is to be a shepherd, a conduit for people to get to their destination, and a guide to accompany them on their journey.

I struggled with this for a while. Why should I use all of my hard-earned money in service of other people's dreams? I have worked, on average, twenty hours a day for the last twenty-four years. That's time away from family that I've spent self-sacrificing, working, learning, networking, and building, trying to be the best version of myself. Sometimes I wondered why I should just keep giving all of these

113

things to people who would most likely betray me or stab me in the back. I eventually came to realize that nothing I have was ever mine in the first place—just the grace of the universe with me as custodian. No matter how hard I work, there is someone working harder. No matter how smart I am, there are many smarter people. It was never about me. It was about grace. I cannot sleep in two beds at the same time or be in two cars at once. So if it belongs to God and I am not going anywhere with it when I die, then why am I reluctant to share it, to empower people with it, to create a better environment with it, to put smiles on people's faces? This realization changed my life forever.

And mine (Kunle's) too. Indeed, if we are not going anywhere with all we have when we die, then why should we be reluctant to share it? I am sure this realization has changed your life as well—either before now or just now in this minute. My father lived according to the same principle Toye just shared—the idea that the meaning of our lives will be represented by the joy and purpose we've unlocked in the lives of others. Probably the greatest struggle of my fifty-plus years on earth is that I pay such a great deal of attention to the advancement of others' causes to my own detriment. I am, however, learning that only he who is well can donate blood. I define this wellness as an endless capacity to show up when and where I need to and be a part of the miracles in the lives of others. Yet as I continue to learn and establish a transferable balance, nothing can match or take away the joy of being able to stand as one Olakunle Soriyan, with the hopes and aspirations of others playing a decisive part in the delivery of the promise of the universe to them. It is a sacred duty I believe in and one from which we cannot look away.

There is an epidemic of inequality around the world, especially in Africa. There is a desperate need for visionaries who look out not only for themselves but also for others. Consider the impact of foundations such as the Rockefeller Foundation, the MacArthur Foundation, the Ford Foundation, the Carnegie Foundation for the Advancement of Teaching, and so many others. These foundations are named after individuals who have been dead for decades but whose legacies still live on through their charitable works. There is too much poverty in Africa and too much inequality. It puts our billionaires to shame. We can do more. We *must* do more so that future generations will be better because we chose to make a difference.

There are countless young people across the continent with the ideas, the energy, and the vision to change Africa. We need to sponsor them. We do not believe in mentorship; we believe in sponsorship. A sponsor is like a parent, someone who holds your hand through difficult times and challenges you to be better but does not judge you for your flaws. It's someone who will walk with you and open doors for you. God uses sponsors to give people favor.

Find people whom you can sponsor. You don't have to be a billionaire to do this. Giving a bottle of water a day to one person in need is actually the beginning of your vision to end lack of water everywhere in the world. Giving an orange once a week to a hungry soul is the beginning of your vision to end food shortage throughout the world. Adding ten dollars a month to the education of a kid in Haiti, Tanzania, or even the house down the street can be the initial expression of your vision to build a world-class university free to its students. It does not take billions of dollars to do good in the world. Goodness is within the reach of every soul committed to directing their God-given will toward magnanimity and benevolence.

The future of Africa depends on the proliferation of people willing to sacrifice personal gain for the collective good. Money and success are meaningless if they do not empower others. Pay it forward. Be your brother's keeper.

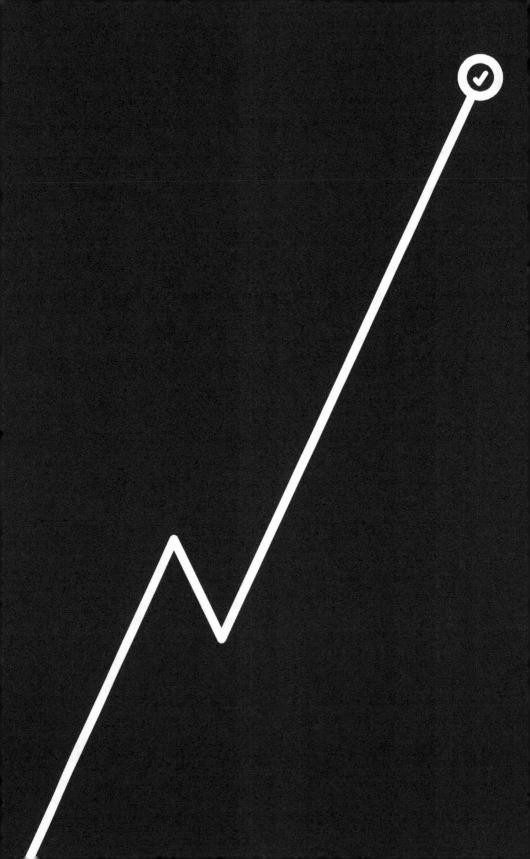

CHAPTER NINE

THE UNSEEN HAND OF GRACE

· ·

It is common to define the factors that contribute to a successful life in terms of what is appraisable. Measurable efforts—such as envisioning, goal setting, hard work, and perseverance—are about input determining output. This makes sense; we get from life what we put into it. But do note that this is only half the story. There is a significant aspect of our desires and pursuits that is left outside our control—our lives themselves. If the next breath we draw is not predictable, then neither are the outcomes of our aspirations.

We exist in a moral universe beyond the full grasp of logical appraisal, one whose arc thankfully bends toward justice. Call it luck, call it chance, call it providence, or call it the X factor. Whatever we call it, we believe in grace and that we are products of it. We believe that the origin of our lives, the ideas we conceive of, and the resources we find along the way all enjoy the interventions of a benevolent universe.

We both attest to the role of grace in our journeys. We are stories of grace, young men from tiny pockets of Nigeria with dreams that transcended borders. It is impossible to draw a straight line from where we came from to where we are now, even though our journey continues. There have been endless detours and failures, setbacks that appeared insurmountable, mistakes, and getting up and trying again until the floor got tired of seeing our backsides, but we grew better with each attempt. Despite all of these difficulties, we can now see clearly the numerous situations we would not have recovered from, the people we would not have met, the opportunities that came from the most unlikely situations, the unexpected flashes of light that gave clarity, and the many timely instances of grace.

Grace should be met with faith. The universe believed in you so much that it gave you life. It gives you many chances to manifest your purpose as long as you draw breath. So why not believe in yourself? God has made a business case for you. Your very breath is proof there is something ahead to touch, feel, and share. You exist with abilities and embody dreams. Your possibilities are infinite.

Faith is total—and, in fact, agnostic. If you believe fiercely enough in a gut instinct, in a gripping idea and its possibility—even when it looks unattainable from a standpoint of available resources—and you hold tenaciously to it in the face of failings and revisions—bam!—it happens. This is as close to a miracle as there is. Receiving God's grace does not mean things will not go wrong. There will be setbacks, mistakes, and betrayals—invisible roadblocks you could not have envisioned that will halt you just as you're accelerating—but there is a rare thing that happens when we shift focus from what is not happening to what has, is, and still can.

Exactly two years ago, I (Toye) chose a new path for my life. It's a path that has tested my every strength, exposed every weakness, and made me question whatever I thought I knew about myself, anyone, or anything. All the assumptions and realities I had built my life upon up until the thirtieth of October 2019 were debunked and thrown from the table. It was a total reset. I was walking into a world and life I only knew in my dreams. It looked like a stupid move. Some questioned my sanity. (I know I did too.) Some rejoiced at my supposed fall to the grass. Most were genuinely concerned for me. You see, while I could see it clearly in my dreams, it did not and could not have made sense to anyone else. It was *my* dream, *my* mission—no one else's.

My life appeared great to others. I had a good family, a terrific job, access to almost anyone I wanted to meet, and a wonderful collection of friends, associates, frenemies, and haters. Life looked pretty good from the outside. But I had a big hole inside of me. I knew I was created for more than this, and it was eating me up. I wanted to do more with my skills. I wanted to be free to express all my strengths, weaknesses, and crazy ideas. I wanted to fly without wings. I didn't see myself as a local player. I wanted to be "glocal." I was willing to give anything to taste that feeling you get when you are taking a major step without knowing the outcome—that animalistic rush of combined fear, anxiety, and excitement.

My loved ones did their best to support me. I remember when I told my dad (God bless his soul) about my decision. It took him all the strength he had left after his ninety-six years on earth to summon the words "It will be well," but the tears in his eye betrayed his true feelings. My mom, family members, and true friends were in a daze, wondering how "we" got here after all the sacrifices I had put into building the life I was now about to let go. But you see, that dream was too tempting, and the voice inside me, which I knew then—and know now more than ever—was the voice of God, told me to jump. God didn't promise me an easy ride. Why would He do that? Even the prophets in the holy books had very colorful rides filled with severe difficulties. Many were jailed, beheaded, declared heretics, and crucified.

But they had God's promise, and I had it too. God promised me a ride, a colorful one indeed, and He assured me He would be by my side. That was all I needed to know to take the leap of faith!

And what a ride it has been since then. I am so grateful for the laughter, tears, support, betrayals, and scars I've endured since I made my decision. Every day in my life is a lifetime. Building my new life has taken me over several mountains and through numerous valleys. I have met real-life superheroes who sacrifice everything for others, and I have come across demons who don't care about anything, including their own souls. I have been blessed with amazing new people in my life, while some people whom I thought I couldn't survive without have left. I lost my confidant and biggest leader, my dad, and gained an angel and many more dads along the way. I walked into a glass door, bloodying myself before being carried away, but I am still walking. Some people are still waiting to see me lying on that grass they imagined would cushion my fall. Well, let them keep waiting! I have made many mistakes and will surely make some more. For anyone whom I may have disappointed, I apologize. I hope I can correct that in this lifetime. For those who have supported me along my journey, God bless you all.

I am a two-year-old version of myself. What we have achieved as a team at Platform is something of which I am extremely proud. What we are going to achieve in the long term is what gets me up every day. Showing that profit, people, planet, and spirituality can coexist and all achieve maximum peaks of success is the dream I was given by my Creator, and I will pursue that dream until my last day on earth.

As authors of this book, our hope is that it will inspire someone experiencing similar doubts about making a seemingly difficult transition to take a leap in faith. Trust what you see *inside* yourself, even if what you see on the outside is not as clear and smooth. There is magic in new beginnings.

Grace is gratitude sensitive. There are so many benefits to remaining thankful that doing so becomes of strategic value. Think of it as a market value activity—a low-cost, high-yield endeavor

Grace is gratitude sensitive.

with practically zero financial spend, something to be deliberate about. In the midst of life's fluctuating gradients of chaos, find something to be thankful for. There is always something. We just tend to be hyperaware of our problems. People who are grateful tend to find grace in other people. Be thankful for the little things—for your parents and partners, for children and the joy they bring to the world, for the person who holds the door open for you to walk through, for the people on your team who make it easier, for your friends, clients, customers, investors, and potential investors. Acknowledge the input of other people. Say "thank you" often, and the universe will send more destiny helpers your way, people who are open to you, your ideas, and your success.

There are numerous studies that show a correlation between gratitude and happiness. In one such study, two psychologists, Dr. Robert A. Emmons of the University of California, Davis, and Dr. Michael E. McCullough of the University of Miami, asked selected participants to write a few sentences each week, focusing on some specific topics. Following is an excerpt from a Harvard Medical School newsletter summarizing the study task and its results:

> One group wrote about things they were grateful for that had occurred during the week. A second group wrote about daily irritations or things that had displeased them, and the third wrote about events that had affected them (with no emphasis on them being positive or negative). After ten

weeks, those who wrote about gratitude were more optimistic and felt better about their lives. Surprisingly, they also exercised more and had fewer visits to physicians than those who focused on sources of aggravation.

At the core of grace is gratitude. And gratitude is more than a statement; it is about thoughts, attitude, and mindset. A grateful being expresses appreciation in everyday actions, thoughts, and activities. The universe has plenty to offer but demands multiplication and reinvestment of those gifts with the clear understanding that the recipient is undeserving, for out of billions, you were chosen. Keep an infinite store of gratitude throughout your journey; it will draw grace to you.

One of the beautiful things about grace is that you are never "down and out," *down* maybe but never *out*. Sometimes grace meets you two minutes before crisis. Other times it will meet you two minutes into the crisis. It may even meet you two minutes after the crisis. Regardless of when, it *will* meet you. It meets you when you are at your wits' end, when you're still falling short after having tried every practical solution to a problem. It meets you in those moments when the only strategy left is to surrender to a higher power. Grace steps into the arena and puts you back in the game. The following is a rather interesting historical illustration of this phenomenon.

The citizens of Feldkirch, Austria, didn't know what to do. Napoleon's massive army was preparing to attack. Soldiers had been spotted on the heights above the little town, which was situated on the Austrian border. A council of citizens was hastily summoned to decide whether they should try to defend themselves or display the white flag of surrender. It happened to be Easter Sunday, and the people had gathered in the local church. The pastor rose and said, "Friends, we have been counting on our own strength, and apparently that has failed. As this is the day of our Lord's resurrection, let us just ring the bells, have our services as usual, and leave the matter in His hands. We know only our weakness and not the power of God to defend us." The council accepted his plan, and the church bells rang. The enemy, hearing the sudden peal, concluded that the Austrian army had arrived during the night to defend the town. Before the service ended, the enemy broke camp and left. Grace.

We believe that grace is the sum total of hard work, faith, mercy, favor, and obedience. We must plan our path to stay within the ethical code of the universe, to be conscious of the effects of our actions on other people and the environment. Modern capitalism is such a high-stakes affair, as moral concerns are often disposable, but there are too many reminders throughout history that show us this is not sustainable. We will be working at cross-purposes with grace if we insist on one-upmanship at the expense of one another. Whatever religious edicts underpin our moralities, whatever personal revelations or workings of conscience, let us follow the inner compasses of our hearts. Let us court grace through obedience.

> Grace is the sum total of hard work, faith, mercy, favor, and obedience.

Recipients of grace as we all are, we have an obligation to pay it forward, to give back to the universe, through service to others what has been freely given to us. This creates a chain of Providence that leads back to us. The idea is not to give because we expect to receive back from people but to give with the knowledge that our enduring legacies will reflect it back to us. Our goal should be to give without expecting anything in return. We should find fulfillment in our having contributed our quota to the promise of the human condition as we give to those who do not have the capacity to give back. This is the spirit of grace. It is mercy. It is kindness. It is faith in the law of the universe. It is favor. And sometimes its principal reward is the privilege of being a conduit, a channel for God to work through, because the journeys of all are all intertwined.

With grace, you will reap where you haven't sown. If you only reap where you've sown, then you are in control and can only go so far because no matter how great you are, you are still limited. You need grace, so never forget to extend it to yourself, just as you extend it to others. Be kind to yourself. Do not beat yourself up over your mistakes. Learn lessons from them and move on. People who waste their time on bad decisions tend to repeat them. Forgiving yourself is permitting grace to envelop you and the work of your hands. Pick yourself up and keep going. You are a beneficiary of an infinite supply of grace.

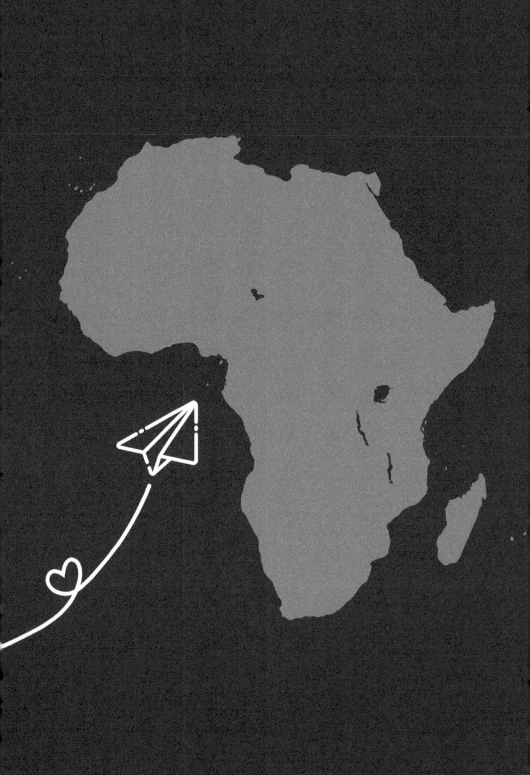

A LOVE LETTER TO AFRICA

. . . .

There has never been a better time than now to be an African. In spite of the injustices faced by people of color all around the world, there has never been a better time to be Black. The pain of the past is real! We've lived through so much: the enduring effects of slavery and colonialism, the decades and decades of bad governance, a legacy of colonization, the stagnation, the squandered potential, the painstakingly slow progress and inability to catch up with the rest of the world. Despite all this, now is the best time to be African and Black. Why do we believe that? Because the future is here, and the future is Black. Nothing can change that; it is inevitable!

The last five hundred years have been painful for Black people across the continent as well as the African diaspora. We who birthed humanity, who developed science and governance, who populated other regions of the world by encouraging migration and supporting both the old and new world with our God-given resources were subjected to slavery, exploitation, ridicule, and pillage. Our glorious histories were obliterated and replaced by dehumanizing narratives that have spurned generations of individuals consumed by self-loathing. There is no one to blame, no need for finger pointing. There is simply responsibility to be taken and a realization of the possibilities and potential the future holds. We must walk into the future with our eyes wide open. The awakening is here. Thanks to the amazing power and exposure of technology, new and vibrant channels of connection and collaboration are opening up between Africans on the continent and the entire African diaspora. We are communicating better with each other, learning from each other, and taking control of our future—slowly but surely.

Righting the errors and mistakes of the last five hundred years won't take ten years. It will take longer. But you know what? With a median age of 19.7, the population of Africa is the youngest in the world. And they are ready. They are coming. As we write this, about 60 percent of Africa's population is younger than twenty-five, and more than one-third are between fifteen and thirty-four. They represent 22.7 percent of the world's youth population. Estimates show that by the year 2100, Africa will still have the youngest population in the world, with a median age of thirty-five. Between 2019 and 2100, Africa's youth population is expected to grow by 181.4 percent, while Europe's is expected to shrink by 21.4 percent and Asia's by 27.7 percent. By 2100 Africa's youth will be equivalent to twice Europe's entire population, and almost one-half of the world's youth will be from Africa.

These young people are acquiring skills at a rate previously unseen. They are connected to the world and to each other. They are innovating, creating solutions, pioneering products, and generating wealth. The first African unicorn—a privately held company with a value of over $1 billion—was created in 2019. Now we have seven, just a few years after the first one. Based on our research, we project another thirteen will be created within the next two years. Still, this is a fraction of the hundreds of global unicorns that have been birthed. We are coming. If you add Africans in the diaspora and people of African descent to that number, we will have over forty unicorns in two years.

These success stories are in addition to our resource-based development potential, of which we still have significant quantities to leverage, from gold, cobalt, and cocoa to cotton, diamonds, and gas. We also have a great deal of arable land and limited natural disasters. But beyond all these, our best resource is our people. They are beautiful, hungry, and skilling up at an unprecedented rate. All 1.4 billion of us (2.5 billion in thirty years, of which 1.1 billion will be members of the working population) are brimming with ideas and the requisite courage to bring them to life. Indeed, the future is Black.

Now if you are not from Africa and lack our genes, we have good news for you. You can be Black too because to be Black is to be your brother's keeper. It's to sow a seed, to collaborate, and to partner. It is to show support and loyalty to ourselves, to our convictions, and to our vision. To be Black is to be authentic. We are real people. Our difference makes us unique. We are capable and competent with unusual capacity and energy. We possess knowledge—knowledge of everything around us and an acute mental alertness. Black is the future. Black is cool. Black is a movement. Black is a vibe.

We are obsessed with Africa, with its beauty, ugliness, diversity, history, failures, and potential. Africa—and Nigeria in particular—gives us a reason to keep going. When things don't work out, as is common in life, we look around and soak in the positive aspects of our current situation, and—voilà—we find the willpower and energy we need to insulate ourselves from the pain. The hope that surrounds us under the African sun keeps us going. Nothing is difficult enough to permanently stop us in our tracks. The possibilities of Africa and Nigeria keep our dreams going. They say that to be successful, you should live 10 percent in the past (so you learn from your decision-making), 20 percent in the present (so you adapt and survive), and 70 percent in the future (so you can create the tomorrow in which you are king and where all is possible). Africa is our 70 percent.

Our tomorrow is about the Africa of our dreams. It's an Africa where everyone is relevant, from teachers to scientists, soccer players to engineers. This is why we invest in all sectors and support entrepreneurs focused on leading the change of our narrative as Africans.

In the last fifteen years, we have witnessed more stability in political and governance structures across the continent with seamless democratic transitions of power—from Nigeria to Ghana, Namibia, and Zambia. In fact, since 2015, we have seen approximately twenty-six leadership changes, showing the flowering of active citizenship and the growing demand for more transparency and accountability in leadership with marked improvements in the rule of law and the defense and upholding of rights. According to the World Health Organization, health indicators, including maternal and infant mortality rates, are also on the decline. Countries across the African continent are on a steady march to meet the United Nations' Sustainable Development Goals by 2030. A 2020 UNESCO report shows that adult literacy rates are up by 10 percent since 1995, and primary school enrollment since 2000 has gone from 60 million to 150 million. Indices on gender equality show that Africa is improving faster than most regions. In eleven countries across the continent, women hold about one-third of the parliament seats, with numbers higher than those in both Europe and the United States of America.

By all accounts Africa is making progress. Our future is synching up with our glorious past, and we are more than delighted to see and be a part of it. We must keep the momentum going. To do this, we must connect ideas to capital faster than they can be conjured.

History has always turned on the fulcrum of ideas. It is the instrument of thought that moved us from caves to skyscrapers, that defined the ethical constructs through which we have self-organized. The French Revolution, whose ripple effects more or less birthed the modern nation-state, was preceded by the Enlightenment, the eighteenth-century movement that championed scientific thought, philosophy, religious tolerance, and democratic ideals such as liberty. In 1848 philosopher and economist Karl Marx released his seminal work *The Communist Manifesto*, a revolutionary idea that captured the imagination of the twentieth century and altered how we thought about leadership, governance, and equality. Centuries before Marx, Martin Luther's Ninety-Five Theses sparked the Protestant Reformation with its far-reaching sociopolitical and economic implications. Behind the Industrial Revolution and its subsequent waves were cultures of scientific inquiry and technological discoveries. Ideas compel us to assess the resources available to us per space, per time, and how much meaningful progress we can create with their innovative deployment.

But ideas are nothing unless they are implemented. Marx's *Communist Manifesto* was idle thought without action. Luther's Ninety-Five Theses was disgruntled gossip without the courageous actions that backed it up. Marx was thirty when he published *The Communist Manifesto*. Luther was thirty-four when he nailed his world-changing theses to the castle church in Wittenberg. Like every revolutionary after them, they risked life and limb to change the world. And they were *young*. This is why we have written this book.

The world we live in today was created by people who took chances, people who were curious and restless enough to investigate and act. Even when they failed, they tried again—tried better. They made a difference. The Africa of the future, which is now unraveling, is locked up in the ideas of the young people in every corner of the continent putting their hands to the plow. Go for your dreams, for all that's in your heart. We are by no means saying we are experts in failure, but what we can tell you, for sure, is that failure is negatively overrated, and you have more to lose by not trying. Young people have so much to offer the world when they dare.

Mark Zuckerberg was a nineteen-year-old Harvard undergrad when he launched Facebook in 2004. Ten months later his dorm experiment had generated about one million active users. Less than a decade later, it had over two billion monthly active users, landing Zuckerberg a net worth, by Forbes estimates, of $34 billion. Of course, he experienced some failures along the way. "We were told to sell our company many times, but I didn't want to," he said. "Slowly, everyone left, and I felt alone. That was my most difficult time while making Facebook. The greatest success comes from the freedom to fail."

There are so many legitimate reasons to despair about the conditions in Africa. We can all sit back and blame our respective governments for all the many ways our affairs have been mismanaged. But this will get us nowhere. Within the debacles that we find in our current existence, innovation beckons. We charge you to seize it. The myriad problems we face present extant opportunities for rewriting the narrative. Ideas come from the observed world, from an open-eyed view of the conditions in which we live and the gaps yawning to be filled. So do not be discouraged by Africa and the very understandable historical challenges we face. Instead, be inspired as we are. Come up with an idea. Think of where you can add value. There is nobody without something to give. Collaborate if you need to. We are stronger and have greater endurance when we work together.

One of the most significant technologies behind many websites today, WordPress, was started by nineteen-year-old Matt Mullenweg in 2003. The company began because the development of an existing blogging software, b2/cafelog, was abandoned by the original developers, leaving a significant gap. In 2003 two users of b2/cafelog, Matt Mullenweg and Mike Little, decided to build a new platform on top of b2/cafelog and keep things going. This idea, derived from the need to fill a need, would go on to become one of the most notable open-source content management systems, dubbed the king of blogs. On May 27, 2003, Matt announced the availability of the first version of WordPress, which received a glowing reception by the community. The collaborators had taken the existing b2/cafelog platform and made significant improvements. They included a new admin interface and new templates and generated XHTML 1.1–compliant templates. Today WordPress is valued at over $1 billion and still growing.

The world we live in today was created by people who not only took chances but also, in spite of the great difficulties that sometimes attend noteworthy efforts, surmounted incredible odds to gift the world something they would forever be remembered for. Louis Braille was blinded by an accident at the age of three. This was France in the nineteenth century, without the technological advancements of today. What should have restricted the young Braille's life instead defined his greatness because he refused to be limited by his disability. At the age of fifteen, he adapted a military messaging system into an embossed dot-reading format for the blind. He went on to publish a number of Braille schoolbooks and, through practice, became an accomplished musician. A century after his death in 1852, Braille's body was exhumed and reburied in the Pantheon in Paris alongside French national heroes in recognition of his achievements.

Our charge is this: come up with an idea and the courage to

implement it, knowing that the inevitable failures you'll face in its pursuit are not a disadvantage but a natural occurrence in the progression of your vision. These failures will contain lessons to propel you further and make you better, stronger, and more informed. No matter the difficulties you face, and you will face many, there is safe landing ahead if you weather the storm. And for this task, we have African entrepreneurs in mind—the brilliant, courageous dreamers and stargazers fighting to advance their dreams. Do not fear failure; embrace it. Your ideas are valid. There will be different iterations of them. Some will prove untenable, but the core of them will survive and thrive to the benefit of many if you stay the course. The truth is Africa needs you.

Your ideas are valid.

Official data estimates about 146 million Africans live abroad. With the population of Africa estimated at around 1.2 billion people, this implies about 12 percent of us live outside of the African continent. Those who make up the 12 percent remitted approximately US$78 billion back to Africa in 2020. A quick arithmetic shows that the remittance per capita is about $534. The per capita remittance of Nigerians is $988 from the estimated 17 million Nigerians living abroad. When we compare these per capita numbers with those of other communities, we see that in the Lebanese community, remittances are $664 per capita. (Of the estimated 17 million Lebanese, about 11 million live in diaspora.) In the Jewish community, remittances are $565 per capita from the United States alone. (Six million Jews live in the United States while 6.9 million Jews live in Israel.) The GDP per capita of Africa is $2,569; Nigeria is $2,097; Lebanon is $4,891; and Israel is $43,610. As we can see, there is a very clear role for the African diaspora beyond remittances.

Our research shows that these other diaspora communities do

a lot more than remit money back home. They are involved in skills development, knowledge transfer, collaborative research and innovation, investment, trade, and product exchange. Africa needs her people who live abroad to do much more than send remittances. From our IT professionals (there are only 716,000 software developers in Africa compared with 628,414 in California alone) to our doctors, scientists, and other professionals, the possibilities that can be unlocked are endless.

Changing the African narrative requires everyone getting involved, home or abroad. Our dignity and future depend on all of us being nation builders. There is little government can do. People build their countries. Look through history. The phenomenal rise of China over the last four decades has been entirely government led. Citizen efforts, home and abroad, have played a significant role. Our governments are a reflection of who we are. The African opportunity is the biggest catch-up story in history. We have more foreigners than Africans investing in our start-ups, companies, and innovations. Let's get the money working that we have put into our bank accounts and under our mattresses. Inflation and devaluation risks of money in bank accounts or at home are not better than business risks of investment in start-ups. While 70 percent of start-ups fail, the 30 percent that succeed compensate for them and deliver real returns that exceed the yield on savings, which is often exposed to inflation and devaluation. We are not asking you *not* to save. Informed and enlightened investment in start-ups, equities, and innovation is savings. Stock gambling isn't investment. Get advice when in doubt. Real return on long-term positions in equity (public and private) outperforms pure savings.

Africans, let's collaborate more, invest in each other, share knowledge, engender skills transfer, and have a more positive mindset about ourselves and our future. Our children deserve our best efforts.

Remember, the future starts today. Start creating the future you want to live in.

There is no nation or continent on earth whose development has been the singular responsibility of government. Nations have developed and prospered because a good government approved by the people and supported by a vibrant private sector made all the difference. This is how we must think in understanding our role in building the Africa that is to come. Everything no longer rises and falls on leadership. Africa is at a critical turning point. To make this turn, its leaders and citizens must now understand that the issues we face were invented by decades of human error, so they can be corrected. We are not a continent at risk or a people endangered. We are a people of hope, a generation of promise. And this is our time.

For the African continent, we are convinced that our love for Africa cannot be divorced from our loyalty to it. We believe that for nations like ours, patriotism must be ideologically articulated, codified, and shared in a way that rents a space in the heads and hearts of citizens. It must be unmistakable by friends and foes everywhere. The goal is an intentional insistence on Africa's rightful place in the world, evidenced by the love and loyalty demonstrated to its tools, traditions, flags, customs, intuitions, families, entrepreneurs, entertainment, and authentic forms of government. Our patriotism is defined not by creed or birthplace but by clarity and purpose, as well as a resolve and a set of actions that penetrate ideals such as self-government, the rule of law, freedom of speech, stewardship of private property, a commitment to productivity through people, and progress through education, innovation, and enterprise. Africa must see this, and Africans must rally around this.

> You are not too young to start and not too old to continue.

Nothing will ever be for us if it is without us. Our right to love Africa, to fight for her dignity and the respect she deserves, is a sacred duty. And so our overriding desire is that a dream is ignited in your heart, that you find the courage to go out and implement it. You are not too young to start and not too old to continue. Be hungry for failure, and you will eat at the table of success. Repeat this as many times as you need to. As long as you are trying, magic can happen. So get up and go! What are you waiting for?

RETOOLING AFRICA—A PRIVATE SECTOR CHALLENGE

· ·

The idea that the future is Africa might have sounded hyperbolic ten years ago. Today it does not. It is written. Africa is the future. We have seen this with our own eyes as we traverse the continent and the African diaspora. There is a strategic positioning, with history coming full circle to the source of all creation. There is a mystery about Africa that has lingered in the popular imagination for as long as humans have lived. It's a forgotten civilization, a cultural treasure trove, a victim of history, an economic basket case littered with failed and failing nation-states, a global underdog at once fighting to rid itself of historical demons and control its own narrative. Indeed, Africa has been in a lengthy battle for its soul, for a reclamation of dignity, for self-organizing systems that cater to its diversity and unlock its economic potential. It has been a battle to ward off foreign exploitation and take back its place in the world. Yet despite its challenges,

Africa has been on the move, and when we say its time has come, it is with much more than hollow optimism.

Individuals below the age of twenty-five represent 60 percent of the African continent's population, making it the youngest continent in the world. Africa is poised to fly on the wings of the spirit of its young people. "Each generation must, out of relative obscurity, discover its mission, fulfill it, or betray it," said famed psychiatrist Frantz Fanon. A flowering of mission-minded young people has arisen in the last two decades, change makers from the creative class and civic space, challenged by the inadequacies of local leadership but not restricted by it. They are a generation plugged into the universe of possibilities available today through technology. They're geographically mobile problem-solvers with a healthy appetite for risk and disregard for the status quo. A palpable potential for greatness has slowly unraveled in the last two decades, Africa's manifest hope.

The turn of the millennium signaled a significant ten-year (2000–2009) drive in a positive direction for many African countries. Structural changes in governance between 1990 and 1999—with most countries transitioning from military dictatorships to democracies—laid the foundation for strong economic growth, led by resource boom, economic diversification, and the adoption of technology, symbolized by the penetration of mobile phones. By 2011 Africa was the world's fastest-growing region. Its share of the global working-age population, which is rapidly urbanizing, was predicted to continue rising for the rest of the century as the rest of the world's declined. Due to the effects of two deep global recessions within the last fifteen years (the global financial crisis in 2007–9 and the pandemic-induced recession that began in February of 2020), the continent's growth has been slowed. Its challenges—poor governance structures, weak infra-structure, intra-industry trade deficiencies, and the like—have persisted, but its manifesting potential has not diminished. To build the Africa of our dreams—as we must and as we have already begun to do—we need to focus on optimizing our competitive advantage.

In the next thirty years, half of the world's working population will be African. By 2070 the world will look to Africa to supply labor. With a working-age population of 1.8 billion, what will determine how quickly we grow is how much we invest in the development of young talent across the continent, connecting ideas to capital as quickly as possible.

> Invest in the development of young talent across the continent, connecting ideas to capital as quickly as possible.

THE EDUCATION CONUNDRUM AND PRIVATE SECTOR CHALLENGE

Everyone acknowledges that human talent is our largest and best resource in Nigeria and on the continent. The question is, are we investing enough in this significant resource? Are we educating them enough? Skilling them? Tooling them? The answer is blowing in the wind.

There are 38 million students in Nigeria (over 204 million students in Africa), with 5 percent in tertiary education, 27 percent in secondary education, and 68 percent in primary education. Within 38 million, 85 percent are in public institutions and 15 percent are in private institutions. The quality of education in these private institutions (across all levels, from primary to university) ranges from basic to decent, with few of them comparable to international institutions. The public schools in Nigeria, as in most parts of Africa, are in shameful states. Children do not have books to read or have enough qualified teachers to teach. Some do not have chairs to sit on or tables to write on. Schools that do have qualified teachers do not have teaching tools and aids. It is utterly disappointing. Nigeria's budget for education (excluding capital expenditure) in 2019 was $1.4 billion ($87 billion in Africa), a figure on par with the $1.3 billion allocated for fuel subsidy, and yet we produce oil. To give a clearer picture, what this means is that the country spends just $36 per student and this in the face of twenty-first-century demands and realities.

When we compare government expenditure on education with what private citizens spend, we better understand what we have always known: that Nigerians are ambitious people who will go to any length to be globally competitive but cannot do it at scale because they are short-circuited by individual economic realities and government abdication of duty. To what extent can the private sector address the issues of scale in this regard, and how urgently must it do so? Consider this. There are currently 90,000 Nigerian students studying abroad and 520,000 African students doing so in total. Of these students, 82 percent are enrolled in tertiary education and 18 percent in primary, secondary, and nondegree education. To make this happen, parents spend $4.1 billion (that is, three times the government's 2020 education budget) on their children's education. This works out to be $46,000 spent per student, showing a huge disparity between what the government is allocating to education in Nigeria and what parents are already spending on educating their children by themselves.

Now let us take a step back. We have about 40 million middle-class Nigerians, with the number at 330 million across the continent of Africa. We have about 30,000 millionaires in Nigeria and about

148,000 throughout Africa. The total wealth controlled by this group in Nigeria is in excess of $120 billion—$920 billion across the continent. This figure excludes our brothers and sisters in the Nigerian and African diaspora. If we assume that 80 percent of the savings and deposits in the Nigerian and African banking system are from middle- to upper-class Nigeria in the formal and informal sectors, it means that $29 billion ($600 billion in Africa) is controlled by this group. Applying an interest rate of 10 percent will result in $2.9 billion in interest ($60 billion in interest in Africa). If we take this 10 percent interest on savings and deposits and collectively invest it in education infrastructure, teachers, books, and necessary tools, it puts into perspective the capacity the private sector has in terms of changing the fortunes of the continent. The problems with government are enormous, and we are well aware of them. We analyze them for breakfast and debate them over late-night drinks. As we continue to push for more and more efficiency and effectiveness in public leadership, there is an urgency that a swelling, agile young population hungry for success presents. We cannot afford to leave it up to the government any longer.

We cannot private-pocket away the problems of Africa. They are too present and existential. We can send our children abroad for school; there is no problem in doing so, but it does lead to its own difficulties. Our educated children will either come back and work for, work with, or hire the children of the people the government has neglected. Or at best, our children will remain abroad to face the psychological, social, and career ceilings their race will force on them. It is a question of survival, really. It is not about legacy or impact or some charity but about the survival and well-being of our children and the future of our society.

The average cost of education across OECD countries is currently $12,800 per student. Using this figure as a basis, it will be possible to add 410,000 additional OECD-level educated students annually in Nigeria (5.3 million across Africa) with relevant technical skills into the job market to work with local organizations or provide services to international offshore companies generating significant revenues. India has done this successfully for call centers and technology at a much lower amount ($100 per student) than the OECD average. Using the Indian average cost of education, the number of additional students in Nigeria with quality education could be increased by 53 million (683 million in Africa). We believe that a private-sector-led model of investment in education will not only reduce the skill gap in Nigeria and drive productivity but will also have a direct impact on the overall economic growth and development while arresting the inequality gap that is growing rapidly in Nigeria and across the continent.

THE CASE FOR ENTREPRENEURSHIP: EACH ONE, REACH ONE, TEACH ONE

Entrepreneurship is the key to unleashing the potential of this huge talent base. Demystifying and encouraging entrepreneurship on a significant scale is the only way we can start leveraging our resources as we shift from a consumption-led economy into production (for local consumption and export) and then to a service and eventually a networked economy.

Entrepreneurship and innovation go hand in hand. By enabling one, you get the other. We believe there are two fundamental types of innovation: business model innovation and technology-driven innovation. While technological innovation is about using new technologies to solve real and latent problems, business model innovation is about adapting, advancing, and/or customizing existing solutions to solve existing demands. Nigeria and Africa need both critically and maybe more business model innovations. Technology-driven innovation has been at the fore of creating today's world and will continue to do so; it is needed. For Africa, though, we must add more business model innovation to it.

We have more mobile phones than decent shoes. We have huge swaths of our population in darkness, hungry, and without adequate shelter or clothing. We need to find sustainable business models that can provide electricity, give every economic agent a roof over their head, and produce and store food. Some countries still import tomatoes, eggs, and even water. In Nigeria we import soccer balls, toothpicks, dental floss, and balloons. These are technologies that already exist with barriers of entry in continued decline. What we need are more entrepreneurs who can find ways of adopting these technologies and products for use at varying scale. The ecosystem is tough and not very encouraging for entrepreneurs in Africa. There are public policy obstacles, infrastructure obstacles, and funding obstacles. But all of these are surmountable. We only have to choose the part we must play, and there is a significant lever we can pull to great result: capital. Stay with us.

In addition to educating, tooling, and scaling entrepreneurs, we need to expose, empower, and encourage them at all levels, from family units to communities, from schools to organizations. Yes, we can advise them, help them think through the issues and risks, but it is critical that we support them. We need to let them know that attempting and failing does not make their dreams less viable. We must share experiences and make introductions where we can. We need to actively raise this consciousness of supporting innovation and entrepreneurship—and, yes, capital.

Despite the availability of capital pools in Nigeria and across Africa, they are not positioned to finance innovation and early-stage entrepreneurial activities for reasons including capital source, government economic policies, data, skill level, etc. This is why we have not seen the type of growth in economic activity that will move the needle in Africa's economic evolution. The consequence of this is that many start-ups, despite the brilliance and drive of so many of them, are unable to make the transition to medium-sized companies because of a paucity of capital. And because we exist in a low-risk culture that has zero tolerance for or understanding of failure, the few successful start-ups that show early signs of promise get to access more capital than they need. This drives valuations up from an equity perspective or, in some cases, creates a poor credit culture, as capital providers scramble to invest or lend to this small pool of success stories.

This is not a sustainable path. The conveyor belt is drying up. We are not creating enough companies or supporting enough microenterprises to innovate and create products that will move us forward. How do we get beyond this? Again, as in the case of education and entrepreneurship, we all need to get involved.

There are 44 million formal micro, small, and medium enterprises (MSMEs) in sub-Saharan Africa and 37 million in Nigeria alone. According to the World Bank, there are 42 million microenterprises (that is, companies with ten employees or fewer) out of the 44 million MSMEs. This ratio of the microenterprises to SMEs presents a telling picture. If we can successfully move 10 million microenterprises to become SMEs, this transition alone could create over 40 million economic agents that are saving, spending, and investing. The positive multiplier effect of this transition on African GDP would be in excess of 45 percent. This will also contribute to sustainable long-term growth.

Almost every African reading this knows a microenterprise—the mom-and-pop shops in your neighborhood, the bakery where you buy fresh bread, the pharmacy where you buy medication, the furniture maker who built your first dining table before you could afford showroom shopping, the mechanic who fixed your car before you bought your brand-new whip. We all know one entrepreneur who has stuck with his or her trade and is reliable, skilled, and honest. Imagine what impact we could create if those of us who can (and many of us can) take that one microenterprise and support it with capital, time, advice, exposure, and encouragement. Imagine if, in addition to investing some money, we were to dedicate some time once a week, maybe on a Saturday, or even one day a month to sitting with a microenterprise owner, passing on some of our knowledge and listening to her. Imagine the benefits of explaining her options to her, from capital sources, the benefits of keeping proper books, and giving employees medical coverage to subscribing to a defined pension contributory scheme and paying taxes. Can you begin to imagine the impact we would be driving?

If we can successfully transition ten million microenterprises into SMEs and they each create four new jobs, resulting in forty million new employees, with each employee earning above the Nigerian minimum wage of $150 per month, we will have successfully placed them in the lower-middle-class bracket of $4–$10 per day. This is a class bracket that is able to pay its taxes, contribute to its pensions, and afford healthcare insurance. The trickle-down effect will be an increase in government revenue through taxes, a decline in unemployment and social unrest, and a collective positive impact on the nation's and continent's economic output. To achieve this desired impact, we assume that ten million individuals, around 25 percent of Nigeria's middle class, actively invest $16,000 in one year ($1,333 per month or a onetime transfer from their savings account) into a microenterprise, resulting in $160 billion of investable capital being unlocked. This $16,000 microinvestment will be utilized to fund salaries ($7,200), capital expenditure ($6,000), and working capital ($2,800). Typically, this money either goes into savings or is spent on sundry items.

There is an exploding number of young start-ups making significant strides across the continent, and there is a gradually corresponding number of investors. Before valuations go through the roof as everyone competes for the limited number of companies that make it through, we need to support this important work by birthing new winners. Investing in start-ups and early-stage businesses can be very profitable. Data points using companies that made the transition successfully from micro to large companies show that early investors make the most (yes, you can also lose it all), but if you invest your money in an enterprise you know well, backing an entrepreneur you are comfortable with, and invest enough time in nurturing this company, I believe the odds are in your favor. They may not all become unicorns, but I'll bet you that some decent swans, cash cows, and gazelles will emerge. Investing in micro and early-stage enterprises is the engine that will drive an educated, skilled, and talented population, where entrepreneurship fueled by innovation delivers the Africa that we all seek.

> As Africans, the willingness to invest in our own dreams, wants, and desire is key to the future we desire, deserve, demand, and must deliver on.

Dignity is a fundamental human right. Choice is dignity's center of gravity. Everyone should have the choice to live the life they want on their own terms. Our understanding of this is that as Africans, the willingness to invest in our own dreams, wants, and desire is key to the future we desire, deserve, demand, and must deliver on. Our dignity as Africans is nonnegotiable, and our commitment to treating each other as we want to be treated on the continent is the catalyst for non-Africans to show us the respect and dignity we deserve. Clearly, on a continent where over 80 percent of us work in informal sectors, creating templates for the informal sector to access finance is critical to our future and dignity. All-inclusive growth is the only way to fully unlock our potential in Africa. All our human resources must be fully optimized for the journey ahead.

We are obsessed with the African narrative, and we believe the only way we can achieve our greatness as Africans and unlock the potential of the continent is by working together as one people. Our belief in the future of Nigeria and Africa is extremely positive. Despite all the negative elements of our current existence and painful history over the last several hundred years (poor governance, suboptimal use of our resources, and wickedness to each other), we see greatness everywhere. The world will turn to Africa for innovative solutions in agriculture, fintech, edutech, and more. We must start now to build the businesses that will meet this demand.

Building a bridge between Africa and the rest of the world is critical to changing the African narrative. We are committed to doing our part. But change does not occur overnight. It takes time, and when you are in the middle of the process, it does not feel like you are changing. The caterpillar metamorphosing into a butterfly can tell better of the difficulties the process might entail, but it emerges beautiful and with wings. The world we live in today took billions of years to form. Even the much-touted modern-day economic success stories—Singapore, China, Dubai—took decades to blossom.

The playbook is about incubation, capital formation, collaboration, skills, and knowledge acquisition, and we are well on our way. We must continue to play our part in creating enabling environments that encourage young people to be part of the dialogue and the solution. By combining global knowledge and capabilities with local opportunities and competencies to create a unique blend of local solutions, we can effectively address the challenges we encounter. No one will build our continent for us. Nation building is our collective responsibility. Our history of failure cannot continue to define the promise of change we owe the future to create. Africa is blessed with deep and robust creative talents and assets, a rich and colorful heritage, captivating stories and storytellers, and an ecosystem of innovators who have continued to deliver world-class output.

Get involved in your community. Lead or support initiatives in education, gender equality, healthcare, entrepreneurship, and other developmental areas. Remember, no matter how wealthy or successful you are, you are poor if your neighbors are poor. If we deliberately and persistently engage, educate, expose, enlighten, and empower our poor, the overall effect on governance and quality of life will be transformational. This is our duty and responsibility.

Anyone who thinks our past as Africans will determine our future has no idea what is coming. Yes, we have significantly underperformed in the past, but our future has never been brighter. We are young. We are acquiring skills, leveraging technology, and trading with one another like never before. We are getting more involved in our governance. We are becoming more vocal. Our priority is our development.

For the young people across the continent with hands on the plow, we see you, and we support you. A harvest is coming. There will be failures and setbacks, days and weeks and months where you feel like giving up. *Do not.* Your magic is just about to happen. Everywhere we turn, Africans are innovating and creating solutions that are not only unlocking value on the continent but also putting the world on notice. Africa is the future. We know it, and the world knows it too. We are coming.

DR. AKINTOYE AKINDELE

ABOUT THE AUTHORS

OLAKUNLE SORIYAN

DR. AKINTOYE AKINDELE

Dr. Akintoye Akindele is a hope merchant, a stargazer, a grace servant, and a permanent student of life. He is the Chairman and CEO of Platform Capital Group, a growth-markets-focused, sector-agnostic investment firm deploying patient, value-accretive capital alongside international and local value investors to create and champion businesses with the potential for regional or global scale.

Dr. Akindele is an investor, best-selling author, and philanthropist committed to enhancing Africa's role in the global economy. His pressing focus is to directly empower one million entrepreneurs across the African continent by 2030. He believes entrepreneurs are the hope and promise of the socioeconomic transformation the continent deserves, and that only as everyday problems of contemporary life are confronted by innovation will Africa unleash its full potential to birth a Cockaigne that will be the pride of the entire human race. He is therefore single-mindedly focused on ideas that can not only scale globally, but also can unlock possibilities and development in cities on the continent, and those authored in digital and technological formats especially.

Dr. Akindele sits on the board of several companies across the world and is a frequent speaker at conferences on various topics. His sessions usually aim to simplify transformation and development for change makers everywhere, particularly those working within his area of greatest passion, which is the socioeconomic transformation and future greatness of the African continent.

Dr. Akintoye Akindele is also the CEO of Duport Midstream Company Limited; Chairman and CEO of Atlantic International Refineries & Petrochemicals Limited; Co-Chairman of Liquidity Club; and Director of Koniku Inc. USA, among others. He is also a lecturer and faculty member of the University of Lagos Business School and Founder of Synergy Capital Managers. He is a CFA Charterholder and earned a doctorate in Business Administration (Finance) from the International School of Management in Paris.

Dr. Akindele lives in Lagos, Nigeria.

OLAKUNLE SORIYAN

For over two decades, Olakunle Soriyan has been birthing newness and next level globally, creating five experiences daily, (1) Helping visionaries become influencers and helping influencers become visionaries; (2) Helping leaders see the future of the world, and supporting them to take their stake in it; (3) Helping individuals and families find their personal meaning and purpose, maximize their humanity, and live out the best version of themselves; (4) Helping high achievers pivot or disrupt their highest accomplishments and birthing their necessary next level of relevance and power; and (5) Helping thought leaders find their voice and spread their message to the exact people and places designed for it, anywhere in the world.

Olakunle Soriyan is the Chief Knowledge Officer and Lead Strategist at KENNETH SORIYAN RESEARCH AND IDEAS LLC. He is also the founder of ESHIRYA-Africa, a US 501(c)(3) Exempt Non-

Profit mobilizing and empowering 1 percent of the African population and people of African descent everywhere to function beyond welfare economics, equipped to take responsibility for their socioeconomic and political destiny to the continent. He is also the CEO of AFRICA HOUSE, a platform linking investors with entrepreneurs and innovators of African descent. Soriyan's skills have served various arms of governments and many organizations in different parts of the world including Fortune 500 companies like Coca-Cola, Microsoft, Total, Shell, and many more.

The Ruckus, as he is called by industry colleagues and stakeholders, wears many hats as a Futurist, Iconoclast, Global Thought Leader, and Global Influence Curator; Culture-Shaper, Philanthropist and Social Impact Investor; Advisor to many high-impact individuals in the world, Mentor and Spiritual Guide to thousands across the globe. His life mission is to impact eighty million Global Action Figures shaping culture and making the world a positive and better place in business, government, media, entertainment, family, education, and faith by 2050 and beyond. As a person of faith, Olakunle Soriyan expresses his authentic call helping Christian Leaders and Ministries understand global relevance, the future of Religion and the Church.

He is happily married to his beautiful wife, Tiwa, and they are both blessed with a son, David. The family lives in Plano, Texas.

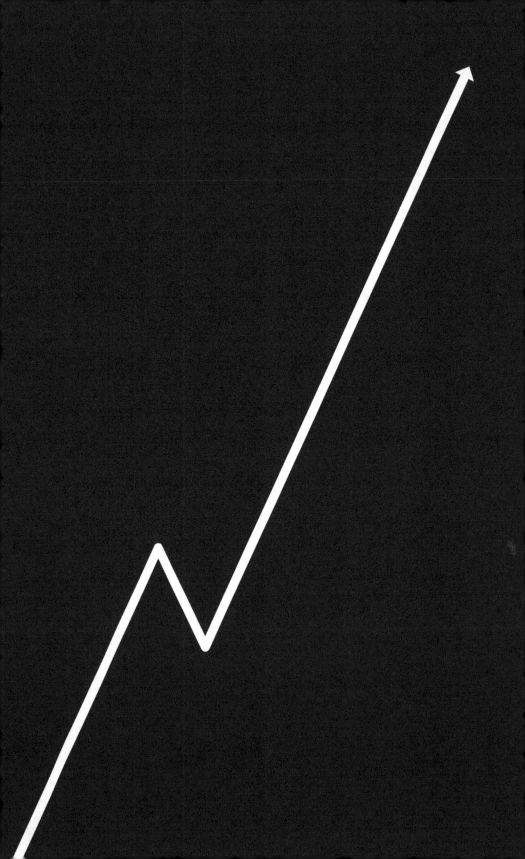

ACKNOWLEDGMENTS

· ·

That efforts are assessed only in measurable terms will be true if a thousand years twice and more is possible as a lifetime; and that all the best of human advancements were curated with the efforts of the collective in how the vision of one or of a few becomes the mission of the many.

We are not exceptions to these as authors.

We acknowledge the patience of family especially, but also of colleagues and friends who endured our nights of fact-finding, writing, and editing. We however must single out our amazing editor, Mr. Efe Azino-Paul, who worked tirelessly in pace and creative strength to match our restlessness to gift our thoughts to the world. Thank you, Efe. Indeed, warrior you are.

We most humbly celebrate and honor the blessed and weighty magnanimous Bishop T.D. Jakes for endorsing our content with his priceless foreword of the book despite his obvious busy schedule. Thank you very much, Bishop. We do not take the kind gesture for granted.

CPSIA information can be obtained
at www.ICGtesting.com
Printed in the USA
JSHW022234200622
27287JS00005B/9